The Solomon Syndrome

The Solomon Syndrome

For Men Who Want More Out of Life

Bob Beltz

Fleming H. Revell
A Division of Baker Book House Co
Grand Rapids, Michigan 49516

© 1995 by Bob Beltz

Published by Fleming H. Revell
a division of Baker Book House Company
P.O. Box 6287, Grand Rapids, MI 49516-6287

Printed in the United States of America

Library of Congress Cataloging-in-Publication Data

Beltz, Bob.
   The Solomon syndrome: for men who want more out of life /
Bob Beltz.
      p. cm.
   Includes bibliographical references.
   ISBN 0-8007-5569-3 (pbk.)
      1. Men—religious life. 2. Self-actualization (Psychology)—Re-
ligious aspects—Christianity. I. Title.
   BV4843.B47 1995
   248.8′42—dc20   95-6507

Contents

Foreword

I t has been nearly fifteen years since I first met Dr. Bob Beltz. I had recently moved to Colorado to take the position of Head Football Coach at the University of Colorado. At the time, Bob and my good friend Bo Mitchell were starting a new church called Cherry Hills Community Church. Bo kept telling me, "Beltz is the greatest Bible teacher in America." I don't know if that is the case, but I can tell you this: Over the last fifteen years I have had the privilege of seeing the lives of a multitude of men influenced for Christ through Bob's teaching ministry.

By the time God raised up the ministry of Promise Keepers, Cherry Hills had grown to over 5,000 members and Bob's weekly men's Bible study had become one of the largest, ongoing men's groups in the nation. Several of our board members and staff are frequent visitors at the study. The group is a model of what I wish was happening in every church in America.

Last year Bob wrote *Daily Disciplines for the Christian Man* as a resource for the ministry of Promise Keepers. It continues to have tremendous impact on the lives of men who read it and put into practice the principles Bob teaches. Now Bob has tackled another critical area of need in *The Solomon Syndrome*.

I first heard Bob speak on this several years ago at a couples retreat that my wife, Lindy, and I attended. Reading the manuscript of the book brought back memories of how critically important are the truths contained here. If there is one area where men today are confused and struggling, it is in the area of priorities and relationships. The message of Bob's book confirms in my heart the very decisions I made this year and the path Almighty God has led me to take. The book not only clearly sets forth the network of relationships God has designed to meet our deepest needs and bring him the greatest glory, it also tells us how to make the changes necessary to build our marriages, our families, our friendships, and most importantly, our relationship with the Lord Jesus Christ.

The Solomon Syndrome. What a great name for the trap that seems to so easily distract us from the things in life that really count. Life is too short to stay entangled in this syndrome. We need help figuring out how to live in a better way. I think Bob has given us that help. He has written a playbook on relationships. This is a book every man who wants to be God's man needs to read!

Bill McCartney

Acknowledgments

I would like to express my deep appreciation to the people who have made this book possible. First and foremost, I am grateful to my wife, Allison, and my children, Stephanie and Baker, for providing the living laboratory in which the heart of this material has been field tested. Many thanks to Bo Mitchell and Everett Dye for inviting me to develop the material on relationships and priorities that we taught together for over ten years in our work with the Executive Network.

I would like to thank Dr. Vernon Grounds and the faculty of Denver Seminary for the role they have played in teaching me to think biblically.

I am deeply indebted to Jim Dixon and the rest of the staff, elders, and members of Cherry Hills Community Church for providing me with a ministry opportunity that enables me to serve in the areas of my giftedness while covering me in the areas of my immense weakness. Special thanks is due Karen Morrison, my administrative assistant, for helping create a bit of *cosmos* in the midst of my *chaos*.

Don Oden generously did my art work again, gratis. Lois Curley wisely put the manuscript into the hands of Bill Petersen, for which I am indebted to her. And finally, as always, thanks to Richard Beach who helped me break out of the Solomon Syndrome by introducing me to Jesus Christ.

To Stephanie and Baker:
For the incomprehensible joy you give!

Introduction

It was a beautiful Friday evening in Colorado. Over fifty thousand people poured into the stadium at Folsom Field on the campus of the University of Colorado. At first glance these facts do not appear to be all that unique. On nearly every Saturday afternoon in the fall of the year this same stadium is filled to capacity with almost that exact number of people. This particular evening, however, was different for two important reasons. On this evening the stadium was filled exclusively with men; more significantly, there was no football team on the field! Those fifty thousand men had gathered together for the National Men's Conference. They had traveled to Boulder to become Promise Keepers.

Walking into the stadium I thought back to a morning nearly six years earlier. My good friend Bo Mitchell had invited me to join him for breakfast with Bill McCartney. Since Bo and I had been working in men's ministry for a number of years, Bill was excited to share with us a vision he believed God had placed on his heart. At the time, Bill, the head coach of the University of Colorado's football team, the Buffalos, was struggling to get his team out of the bottom of the Big Eight standings. I remember my reaction when the coach shared his vision of the stadium in Boulder being filled with fifty thousand men praising the name of Jesus Christ. The skeptic in me was silently thinking, "That's about as likely as the Buffs going to the Orange Bowl!"

There is only one sure way to know whether a vision is given by God. If it comes from God, he will bring it to pass. During the years since that breakfast meeting, Coach Mc-Cartney has led the University of Colorado football team to two Big Eight championships, two visits to the Orange Bowl, and one national championship. But I believe the greatest thrill of the last five years for Bill McCartney came on Friday night, July 30, 1993, when God confirmed Coach McCartney's vision as men from every state and many foreign nations filled the stadium in Boulder.

I was so moved by the experience I decided to bring my son back the next day. On Saturday morning I rode back to Boulder from Denver on my Harley-Davidson. It was a perfect morning for a ride, and my seven-year-old son, Baker, rode behind me holding on for dear life. Riding along the foothills of the Rockies, with my son's arms wrapped around me and his small body pressed against my back, I thought of all the little boys and girls across America whose lives were going to be blessed because their fathers were sitting in that stadium toward which we were heading.

As Baker and I walked through the crowd, we stopped and greeted many friends who had come to the conference. I was excited about my son having the experience of being with this many men who were committed to Jesus Christ. I knew he might not understand the messages being given that morning, so I attempted to explain the event to him in terms he could understand: "Baker, Jesus is helping all these men become better daddies." I knew he got the message when he looked up at me with his toothless seven-year-old grin and exclaimed, "Cool, Dad!"

Men Who Want More

Something exciting is happening in the world today. The phenomenon of Promise Keepers is one very visible expression of it. Men are ready for a change. Many of the men who poured into Folsom Field came to Boulder as believers but left for home as disciples. There ought not to be a difference. But for too many men, I fear, Jesus Christ is only a part of their portfolio and not Lord of their lives. What happened in Boulder is part of a larger movement of God's Spirit in the world today. Christ is calling men to a deeper commitment to himself. The message of the hour is "Come, *follow* me" (Matt. 4:19, italics mine). Men of spiritual sensitivity take that call seriously. It becomes their highest priority.

These men are seeing their lives transformed. For many it begins with their marriages. They remember the day they stood in the presence of friends and family and made a holy vow to love, honor, cherish, and care for their wives until "death do us part." With Christ as their new highest priority, they are working hard to obey the instruction of Jesus to love their wives like Christ loved the church (Eph. 5:23–25).

Looking out over the stadium that evening, I observed a striking phenomenon. As the sun was setting, small flickers of light flashed all over the stadium. At first it appeared as if thousands of the men had "flicked their Bics" like teens at a rock concert. Upon closer examination I realized these small "sparks" were actually being produced by the setting sun as it reflected off the plastic name tags of the men. Many of the men were wearing those name tags over their hearts. The sun's reflection seemed to symbolize the sparks being rekindled in the hearts of those men to love their wives in the way that could only be accomplished by the empowering "fire" of the Holy Spirit.

This is what it means to be a man, a man who wants more out of life and is willing to work to bring his priorities into conformity with God's will. Such a man is committed to Christ, his marriage, his children, his friends, and his fellowman. He is a man who is becoming a living reminder that the real purpose of life is found in the priorities of loving and serving Christ and his fellowman.

The final session of the conference was presided over by Coach McCartney himself. Fifty thousand men had the opportunity to experience what it must feel like to sit in the locker room minutes before game time when the coach stands to give his team their final challenge. But this was no pep talk about winning a game; this was a call to arms. War was declared that night in Boulder.

Coach McCartney reminded the men that a Promise Keeper is a man committed to following Jesus Christ as his personal Commander-in-Chief. He is a man who is ready to "fight the good fight." The battle cry was sounded to begin the War of Love. Fifty thousand men left that stadium ready to go into action as instruments of God's love and peace in a world broken and fragmented by the effects of sin.

Becoming God's Man

You might feel discouraged that you missed this wonderful event in Colorado. Take heart! You don't have to wait for a conference to become a man who lives life to its fullest. You can become a part of this movement of God today by learning how to develop a set of biblical priorities and by investing the time and energy required to build this network of divinely designed relationships. You can learn how to break out of what I call the Solomon Syndrome.

Part One

Beliefs, Boulevards, and Broken Dreams

A Guide to Assessment

1

Boulevard of Broken Dreams

An Introduction to the Solomon Syndrome

Whenever I am in need of a little emotional boost I pack my wife and kids into the family car and head toward Gunther Toody's. Toody's is one of those trendy fifties restaurants where you can still get a big, greasy cheeseburger. The waitresses all dress in fifties garb while the jukebox cranks out an endless stream of golden oldies. In the room where I like to eat, a perfectly restored 1959 Corvette convertible hangs from the ceiling and an eerie print adorns one wall. The print is a modification of a famous painting by Edward Hopper entitled *Nighthawks*. Painted in 1942, *Nighthawks* portrays a late-night scene at a lonely diner. Two men and a woman sit at the counter while another man waits on them behind it. In the Hopper painting the occupants of the diner are unidentifiable.

Several years ago, an artist by the name of Helnwein took the Hopper painting and made a few modifications.

In the Helnwein version we see the same late-night scene and the same diner, but now seated at the counter are James Dean, Humphrey Bogart, and Marilyn Monroe, while behind the counter stands none other than Elvis Presley. Helnwein entitled his work *Boulevard of Broken Dreams.*

I like looking at the print with my wife and children nearby. It reminds me that even though I haven't quite achieved the American dream, maybe that dream isn't all it's cracked up to be. What did these four stars have in common? They all wanted to live full and happy lives. They wanted to feel good about themselves and about what they did. They all had a dream. They all pursued their dreams with passion. Unlike most men and women in the world today, these four achieved their dream. In the end, however, the dream ended up being a broken dream. All died tragically and, in at least three cases, with great disillusionment.

I often find myself looking at the picture and asking the question "What went wrong?" Why is it that so many of our dreams don't bring lasting happiness? The stories of the four people in the picture are certainly not unique. The pages of history are filled with the accounts of men and women who appear to have lived lives of great success and yet were desperately unhappy. You would think that we would get the message. Something is radically wrong! Our culture's definitions of the meaning of life and the way to be happy are defective. The path to happiness, contentment, fulfillment, and satisfaction is not the road of power, possessions, wealth, fame, and prestige. That road is usually a boulevard of broken dreams.

For some reason it is very difficult to remember that the important things in life are often the things upon which our culture does not place great value. I am a rich man, though my bank account might not impress you. As I look at that Helnwein print, however, I am reminded of what is really important. I know what it takes to live in a way that offers an alternative to the despair and disillusionment represented by that work of art. There is a way of life that is characterized by a sense of harmony, contentment, and fulfillment. Discovering this new way requires a change in the way we look at life. This change begins by understanding the Solomon Syndrome.

Bad Theology

Ignatius J. Reilly is the central character in the Pulitzer prize-winning novel *A Confederacy of Dunces*.[1] He is one of those off-center characters who marches to the beat of a different drummer. In the opening chapter of the novel Ignatius is standing in front of a department store observing the apparel of the men and women entering and departing. Spotting a woman dressed in a new and obviously expensive outfit, he makes the assessment that this is a person who lacks a sense of what Ignatius refers to as "good geometry and theology."

Ignatius himself is attired in an outfit that would best be described as "early Goodwill." His oversized corduroy slacks provide plenty of room for his even more oversized torso. His plaid flannel shirt and muffler shield his body so effectively that a coat is not required even though it is the dead of winter. The *pièce de résistance* of the outfit is a bright red hunting cap, fully equipped with built-in earflaps; the earflaps are down, of course. The outfit reflects what Ignatius would classify as both good geometry and good theology.

In the world according to Ignatius J. Reilly, most problems are the result of bad theology (and geometry). Whether or not we would agree with the "theology" of *A Confederacy of Dunces*, one thing is clearly accurate about the observations made in the book: Bad theology can ruin your life.

Perhaps you have never realized that you have a personal theology. We all have belief systems that shape the decisions we make and steer the course of our lives. Your belief system is the foundation of your personal philosophy of life. These deeply ingrained convictions guide the choices, attitudes, and behaviors that shape your life. Your belief system is comprised of all the conscious and unconscious assumptions and beliefs you hold about how your personal needs are going to be met and what will make you happy.

Have you ever known anyone who seemed driven to make money? Our society is filled with people who appear to have this goal as their primary passion. If you could get inside that funny gray matter contained within their skulls, what would you find?

Later I will go into some detail, describing the inner dynamics of the human motivational system. For now, let me simply state that such a money-driven person has exactly the same needs as you and I. His real needs are unconditional love and significance. Real needs are not always consciously known. They are often confused with what have been identified as felt needs. There is a critical difference between the two (which we will also explore in future chapters), but both are filtered through an internal set of beliefs about life and self.

Somewhere along the line the money-driven person developed a belief system (perhaps not fully conscious) that the accumulation of money will meet his needs and make him happy. It is that basic assumption about how to get his needs met that has led to a lifestyle driven by the pursuit of money. Behavior is driven by belief, which in turn is rooted in needs.

In the coming chapters I will show that our real needs are universally the same. Our beliefs and behaviors are as different as our individual experiences and convictions. Our behaviors are shaped by our goals, which are generated by our belief systems—our personal theology. Our behavior will produce outcomes that will either meet our deepest needs or fail to meet these needs. If our needs are met, our lives will be meaningful, fulfilling, and personally satisfying. If, on the other hand, the outcomes we achieve fail to meet our real needs, our lives will be frustrating, depressing, and filled with the vague sense that something is missing. A diagram of the above sequence would look like this:

Dynamics of Human Motivation

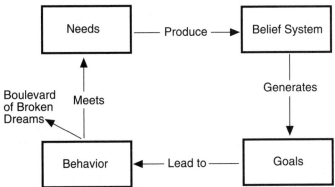

Faulty beliefs (bad theology) will lead to unfulfilling outcomes and unhappy lives! Most men in our society operate with a defective belief system. Our culture has effectively convinced most men that some combination of wealth, power, prestige, and possessions will produce happiness, constituting what both Ignatius J. Reilly and Jesus Christ would call bad theology.

The Solomon Syndrome

Let's create a character much like one of the occupants of Helnwein's diner and attempt to answer that elusive question "What went wrong?"

Think of a sweet little girl growing up in Southern California. By cultural standards she is an exceptionally pretty little girl. All the attention and admiration she receives is based on her appearance. She receives false messages that will translate into her personal belief system as "Beauty earns security and significance."

She becomes enamored with the lives of the men and women she sees on the silver screen at the local movie theater. She reads the manufactured stories of their glamorous lives reported in the movie magazines she buys at the corner drugstore. Her belief system begins to develop further: "Beauty can lead to fame. Fame can give even more security and significance."

As her belief system continues to form, she gives no thought to the fact that what our culture defines as beauty fades and that fame is fleeting. She sees the fur coats and extravagant homes of the rich and famous and adds another component to her belief system: "Fame leads to fortune. Fortune buys even more security and significance."

By the time she reaches young adulthood, her belief system is nearly intact. A photographer notices her beauty and offers to give her the first "break." In the midst of a normal photograph session, he convinces her to pose in the nude. Acquiescing, she might begin to experience the first costs of her faulty belief system; perhaps she feels used. Maybe she feels guilty. Unfortunately, the rapid acceleration toward fame and fortune produced by the photographs neutralizes those feelings, and the photographs open the door to a major studio screen test.

Let's fast-forward our story a bit. Fifteen or twenty years go by. Her beauty has been "enhanced" by bleached hair, expensive clothes, and a great deal of makeup. A change of name has accompanied the extraordinary fame she has experienced. Her fortune has allowed her to acquire anything money can buy. Her goals, based on her belief system, have been fully realized. The critical question becomes "Have her real needs been met?"

There is more to this picture than at first meets the eye. Since she never developed the ability to form lasting relationships based on a foundation other than her beauty, fame, and fortune, her life has been characterized by a string of painful, broken relationships. Fame and fortune cannot fill the void in her life, so she tries to anesthetize her pain with prescription drugs and alcohol. Yet, rather than easing the pain, her behavior only widens the void and increases the pain.

Finally, the staggering reality of aging begins to dawn on her. Wrinkles begin to appear. She begins to gain weight. Sleepless nights and alcohol-induced stupors take their toll. The foundations of her belief system are crumbling. In one final act of desperation she ends her life with an overdose of sleeping pills. Good-bye, Norma Jean!

Norma Jean, better known as Marilyn Monroe, was a classic victim of what I call the Solomon Syndrome. It is one of the most prevalent philosophies of life in our world today. It always, ultimately, leads a person down the Boulevard of Broken Dreams. It is a philosophy of life as old as civilization itself. It is called the Solomon Syndrome because it was never more perfectly expressed than in the life of the third king of the United Kingdom of Israel.

Much of what God attempts to accomplish by giving us a written record of the redemptive history of his people is the impartation of a bit of perspective. This is one of the primary reasons God preserved a piece of the life and teaching of the man named Solomon.

Solomon is a perfect example of what happens when a man loses perspective and deviates from the divine blueprint. Alternatives to the blueprint can be incredibly appealing. A good friend of mine coined the expression "the world's menu" to capture the appeal of the multitude of choices that we face each and every day of our lives.

It used to be relatively easy to order lunch at McDonald's. You either ate a hamburger, a cheeseburger, or a fish sandwich. McDonald's has added more items to the menu, so it takes a bit more thought now. When you eat at a more sophisticated restaurant you often face a dizzying multitude of choices. Life in our culture offers an incredibly diverse "menu." As a result, the quality of perspective becomes even more crucial. Without an accurate perspective on life we can spend years pursuing choices on the menu that simply aren't fulfilling. Solomon has much to teach us in this regard.

Solomon was the son of King David. When David turned the throne of Israel over to his son, the nation was at the beginning of its golden age. Solomon ruled Israel for forty years. They were years of peace and prosperity for the nation of Israel and for Solomon. It appeared that Solomon was a guy who had everything going for him.

Yet at the height of his career, Solomon "hit the wall." From his unique vantage point he wrote a personal reflection on the detours and dead-ends of life. This short reflection is preserved for us in the Bible under the title Ecclesiastes.

Power

In this short book Solomon makes a series of statements regarding his accomplishments. He follows each statement with an assessment of the accomplishment. He begins the treatise with the statement that he is the king in Jerusalem (Eccles. 1:1). This was a man who possessed great political power. We live in a world that teaches us that power will give our lives significance. There is perhaps no greater symbol of power than the throne of a monarch. Solomon occupied such a throne at the pinnacle of his nation's glory.

He wielded power over the lives and affairs of men and nations. Many men and women have lived and died in the pursuit of this kind of power. Even today people will go to almost any sacrifice and expense to gain public office so that they might exercise political power. For many this quest has purely altruistic motives. But the biographies of power-hungry people often lead one to believe that this drive for power is often rooted in a man or woman's basic need for significance. The quest for power becomes an attempt to satisfy a need. Is it possible to satisfy this need with political, economic, or military power? Let's look at Solomon's assessment of his situation.

The Solomon Syndrome

In the opening statement of Ecclesiastes, Solomon makes a rather dismal assessment of the state of his emotional life. His often repeated formula reads, "Vanity of vanities; all is vanity" (Eccles. 1:2 KJV). I like the way the New International Version translates it: "Meaningless! Meaningless! . . . Utterly meaningless! Everything is meaningless." Solomon's message is clear: Even if we reach the pinnacles of power our lives will not be fulfilled if power is an end in and of itself.

Pleasure

Solomon's position enabled him to pursue another path in his quest for personal fulfillment. When power didn't do it, he became a hedonist. His belief system shifted to: "Eat, drink, and be merry." Solomon was quite a modern man in this regard. The main difference between Solomon and Joe Cool at the local single's bar is that Solomon had the ability to pursue pleasure in a way, and to a degree, that few of us could ever match.

The Solomon Syndrome

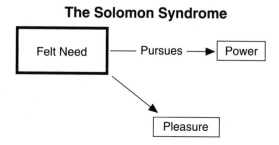

Solomon could honestly say, "I denied myself nothing my eyes desired" (Eccles. 2:10). He tested his heart with pleasure, filled his belly with wine, and kept a harem of three hundred concubines to meet his sexual desires when his seven hundred wives bored him. This was a guy who really understood the meaning of the old adage "wine, women, and song!"

What was his assessment of this pursuit? "Everything was meaningless, a chasing after the wind" (Eccles. 2:11). Pleasure did not fill the void created by the deep need for love and meaning. "Fun" can numb the pain for a while, but it is not a lasting solution to the quest for personal fulfillment.

Possessions

When power and pleasure don't fill the void, what do you turn to next? For Solomon it was possessions. George Carlin, the irreverent comedian and astute observer of human behavior, loves to talk about our culture's obsession with "stuff." Carlin points out that at some time in our lives we all start out with very little stuff. As we grow older we have the tendency to begin to accumulate stuff. Pretty soon we have so much stuff that we have to build a house. What is a house? It is a place where you keep your stuff. Sometimes, after we have lived in a house for a while, we have so much stuff that we have to go and find a bigger house to keep all our stuff in. Pretty soon we have basements, closets, attics, and garages filled with, you guessed it, stuff!

The Solomon Syndrome

I remember when I graduated from college and left home to begin my first job. I drove a little yellow Volkswagen in those days. All my "stuff" fit right in my car. After a few years away from home I met my wife, Allison. We got married. That's when you really begin to accumulate stuff! We spent the first years of married life living in the middle of Nebraska. On weekends our favorite activity was to go to farm auctions. An auction, of course, is a place where you can buy stuff other people don't have room for any more.

When we finally moved from our first little house and went to another job in another city, we still had a little Volkswagen. But this time we had to pull a trailer behind it to move all our stuff. The next time we moved, it took a truck to move our stuff. On our last move, we needed to make two trips with the truck. We have really accumulated a lot of stuff!

As much stuff as we have, it fades in comparison with Solomon's stuff. He had palaces, stables, gardens, parks, and storehouses filled with stuff. He owned flocks, slaves, chariots, and all kinds of great stuff. Did it satisfy his deep needs? Once again his assessment of the situation was "meaningless" (Eccles. 2:11).

Wealth

If there is one predominant message that men in Western culture have adopted as part of their belief system it is that money makes us happy. Solomon was a man who amassed great wealth. There are several passages in the Old Testament that give us information regarding Solomon's wealth. One day I began to calculate his annual income. As I put these pieces together I discovered that Solomon's annual income was somewhere, conservatively speaking, in the range of one-half billion dollars a year, tax free. In 1000 B.C. that kind of cash went a long way! That flow of income continued for over forty years, giving Solomon a net worth of over twenty billion dollars, not counting his real estate holdings. By all standards, he was the wealthiest man on the face of the earth. Here is his assessment of his wealth:

> Whoever loves money never has money enough; whoever loves wealth is never satisfied with his income. This too is meaningless (Eccles. 5:10).

When our life is built around the pursuit of money, the end will certainly be frustration. Part of the tragedy of this pursuit lies in the fact that by the time we figure out its futility it is often too late to concentrate on the things that truly give meaning and purpose to life. The cost of the pursuit of wealth is often found in the destruction of the relationships that really do matter.

The Solomon Syndrome

Education

We also live in a society preoccupied with information. Some humanists believe that the ultimate destiny of mankind hinges on the education of the global village. They think the answers to the dilemmas that face humanity are locked away in the human brain waiting to be freed by the educational process. Yet in the most highly educated society in human history, many of the most highly educated people are the most miserable.

Solomon was no exception. In addition to being powerful and wealthy, he was brilliant. In his early years, before he experienced the disillusionment reflected in Ecclesiastes, Solomon had a marvelous encounter with God. One night God appeared to him and offered him an envious opportunity: "Ask for whatever you want me to give you" (2 Chron. 1:7). In one of those rare moments of clarity that seem to come too infrequently in life, Solomon made a request reflecting a completely unselfish motivation. "Give me wisdom and knowledge," he said, "that I may lead this people, for who is able to govern this great people of yours?" (2 Chron. 1:10).

The Solomon Syndrome

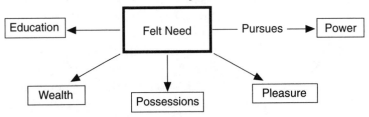

God was pleased with Solomon's request. He not only granted the request, he added to it wealth, honor, and riches (2 Chron. 1:12). Solomon's intellectual capabilities became world famous. People from all over the known world traveled to Jerusalem just to listen to the wisdom of Solomon. If education were the key to personal fulfillment, Solomon would have been a very happy man. Yet, when we look at his assessment of his great wisdom we read, "What then do I gain by being wise? . . . This too is meaningless" (Eccles. 2:15).

Think about it! Every element of the belief system advocated by contemporary culture as the pathway to the good life was fully achieved and experienced by this man. He accomplished the goals of which most people only dream. What did he find? He discovered that for years he had been traveling down the Boulevard of Broken Dreams. The achievement of his goals produced nothing but futility. His real needs were not met.

How many people do you know who are trapped in the Solomon Syndrome? Multitudes of men will spend the limited years of their lives pursuing goals that will never meet their needs.

At the end of his reflection Solomon draws a couple of poignant conclusions about escaping this syndrome. The last chapter of Ecclesiastes begins with his advice to "Remember your Creator in the days of your youth" (Eccles. 12:1). We could paraphrase this advice by affirming that real meaning and purpose in life will only be found in a spiritual solution to life's challenges. Solomon concludes his discourse by saying, "Now all has been heard; here is the conclusion of the matter: Fear God and keep his commandments" (Eccles. 12:13).

How can you break out of the Solomon Syndrome? Let Solomon himself tell you: Assess and adjust! Through Solomon we are challenged to reevaluate our belief systems and the behaviors generated by our philosophy of life. Do we have some bad theology? If we reached our goals would they really bring the fulfillment that meeting our deep needs for security and significance brings?

If you realize that you are trapped in the Solomon Syndrome, you can change. Faulty belief systems can be replaced with a philosophy of life based on truth. It will require some work on your part. In the following chapters I am going to take you on an inward adventure. I hope to help you understand how you got trapped in the syndrome and how to make the necessary changes to your "geometry and theology" that will keep you off the Boulevard of Broken Dreams and move you into a way of living that leads to fulfillment and true happiness.

Personal Reflection

In the coming chapters I will show you how to take some specific steps to break out of the Solomon Syndrome and get your life into harmony with the divine blueprint. Before you move on, you might find it helpful to stop and think about a few questions:

1. What are some of your basic assumptions about life?
2. How much of your current belief system is faulty?
3. In what ways are you caught up in the Solomon Syndrome?
4. Do you want God's best for your life?
5. Are you willing to change?

2

Life's Too Short to Drive a Chevy

And Other Guidelines for Intentional Living

The minute I saw it I had to have it: a T-shirt sporting the Porsche logo in large bold letters across the front of the shirt. Underneath the logo, in freestyle lettering, the shirt declared, "Life's too short to drive a Chevy." Don't get me wrong. I have nothing against Chevrolets or any other make of car. But as a rather committed Porsche enthusiast, I knew exactly what the creator of the shirt was attempting to communicate.

The shirt was more of a statement about one's philosophy of life than a critique of General Motors. Many people go through life driving Chevrolets and are perfectly content. Others negotiate the years harboring a secret desire to own a vehicle like a Porsche. They find themselves experiencing sensations of envy every time they pull up to a stoplight next to some sharp little masterpiece of German engineering. In the back of their minds they are always thinking, "Someday, I'll own one of those." It just seems like that elusive "someday" never arrives.

Life is like that. Life is short. As a matter of fact, life is too short. Too short to drive a Chevy? Maybe, if a Chevy becomes the symbol of missing all the gusto. It is certainly too short to allow many of the really important issues of life to slide by. How can we be sure we don't miss the precious gifts life has to offer? What are the areas of life that deserve our concentration and effort? What makes life worth living? What gives life purpose and meaning? How can we make the adjustments necessary to get more out of life?

Intentional Living

A few years ago John Denver recorded a clever little song about making some radical changes in your life. In the chorus of the song Denver encouraged listeners to blow up their T.V.s, throw away their newspapers, and move to the country.[1]

The song had a special appeal to people who longed to escape the rat race. It reminded us that life is too short to live in bondage to a lifestyle that can never deliver what it promises. Many people live in bondage, and some even recognize that they are in bondage. Few know how to get free.

There are two radically different approaches to living. One is manipulated living, characterized by the man who does not have control over his own life. The term "rat race" is often used to describe this way of living. People whose lives are manipulated seldom experience a great deal of personal fulfillment. What they usually experience is a kind of bondage.

The other style of living is more intentional. Intentional living is making conscious choices about the way we live; it is usually based on certain principles or values. A man who is living intentionally will either be found leading the race or refusing to run; he has a sense that he is in control of his destiny. If we are going to experience life in all its fullness, we must learn to live intentionally. We must also have the correct set of values and principles as the basis of our intentionality.

Both manipulated living and intentional living are products of the same series of dynamics that are basic to all human behavior. Our behavior is the product of the choices we make about how we will live. The sum of these choices creates our lifestyle. Adjustment is the process whereby an individual intentionally makes a series of choices and undertakes a plan of action to redefine and reshape his or her lifestyle.

The adjustment process begins by clarifying the underlying needs that motivate our behavior. We respond to our needs, as we understand them, by adopting certain beliefs about how our needs will be met. In the previous chapter we identified the fact that many of us have adopted belief systems that are in need of radical change. Our belief systems are manifested in a series of choices and actions designed to pursue the goals which we believe will lead to the fulfillment of our felt needs. The outcomes of our choices and behavior determine our existing lifestyles.

In order to move to a more intentional lifestyle we must be able to identify the structure that is already in place. Our lifestyles are made up of three primary building blocks. We each have a certain amount of time, energy, and money to invest in the choices we make about how we will live our lives. An analysis of these resources will reveal what our existing life structure looks like. It is this life structure that actually identifies our philosophy of life.

If you were to ask about my philosophy of life, I could easily articulate a sequence of relational priorities to which I am committed. Conceptually, I have my life well-ordered. Pragmatically, I have a bit of a problem living out what I have developed conceptually. If you want to know about my real philosophy of life, simply evaluate the percentage of my primary resources I invest in those different areas of priority.

Evaluating the use of my resources will also reveal the extent to which I am living intentionally (versus manipulatively). The amount of discrepancy between those things I say are my priorities and my investment of time, energy, and money reveals the extent to which I operate under manipulation.

Even if my resources are invested consistently with my priorities, I still need to determine whether the priorities of my life fit with the priority structure God designed. The two questions each of us must face in making assessments and adjustments are: (1) Am I in bondage to a lifestyle that is running me? and (2) Am I intentionally creating a lifestyle that is out of harmony with God's best for my life?

Someday I will have to make a decision. Has the pursuit of my goals really met the deep needs of my life? Do I feel good about my life and myself as a result of the belief system I have followed, the values I have adopted, and the choices I have made? The answer to these questions can mark the beginning of a major transition time in our lives.

Students of human behavior have discovered that these periods of evaluation and transition often lead to times of crisis in the adult life cycle. An unsatisfactory evaluation can lead to changes in career, marriage, geography, or something else in an attempt to get needs met. Without an accompanying change in our belief system, these transitions become no more than brief detours that ultimately lead back to the Boulevard of Broken Dreams. After a series of these transitions, life begins to wind down and we are suddenly faced with the fact that life is too short and somehow we have wasted it. But that need not be the case.

"Protest Against the Rising Tide of Conformity"

Change is difficult. We tend to lock into behavior patterns that become habits. Often these habits and the belief systems that lie behind them are extremely complex in their origins. They are a product of the constant bombardment of the *zeitgeist* (spirit of the age) and the dynamics of personality development that have shaped our lives. When these dynamics lead us to buy into the prevailing value system of the culture and respond with corresponding behavior, we become locked into conformity.

Recently I decided it was time for a new family photo. We had not had one taken in several years, and I wanted to do something a little different. A good friend of mine, Ken Bisio, is a well-known professional photographer. His work hangs in some of the better galleries in the States and abroad. I called Ken and asked if he would "shoot" our family in a kind of funky family photo. Ken told me he knew just the spot and directed us to meet him at an abandoned warehouse in lower downtown Denver, an area known locally as "Lo-Do."

Our whole family dressed in our motorcycle gear and headed for Lo-Do. My wife, Ali, and daughter, Stephanie, drove the car while my son, Baker, and I rode my Harley. When we arrived at the warehouse we immediately knew why Ken picked that particular spot. Spray-painted on the warehouse door was the graffiti challenge "Protest Against the Rising Tide of Conformity." We all assumed a Harley attitude and Ken captured the scene on Kodachrome. The "family portrait" came out great.

The message painted on that warehouse door is a critical one for many men in America. The time has come to protest against conformity to a defective cultural belief system; it is time to break out of a manipulated lifestyle, to reverse the Solomon Syndrome. The big question becomes "How do we do it?"

Nearly two thousand years ago, a man named Jesus gave a formula for making the break. "You will know the truth, and the truth will set you free" (John 8:32). These words of Jesus contain a formula for breaking out of bondage and moving into a life of freedom. Jesus Christ is a liberator. He liberates in a multitude of ways. One of the more exciting ways he liberates is in this area of breaking free from defective belief systems and unfulfilling lifestyles.

The formula was preceded by a condition, a prerequisite for experiencing the liberating power of Jesus. "If you hold to my teaching," Jesus said, "you are really my disciples" (John 8:31). The prerequisite for freedom is a willingness to change. We must recognize that our definition of our needs and our belief system about how they will be met might be faulty. This is not easy because it requires what the Bible calls humility. Our natural tendency is to justify and rationalize our lives. By nature we are more prideful and stubborn than humble. Openness to change is a big step in the right direction.

Once we have taken the step of openness to change we must be willing to accept a new source of authority. If we are going to experience true liberty our new authority on life must now become the author of life himself. We need to find out if God has anything to say about our needs and how to meet them. His revealed truth needs to become the basis of our belief system. We must then attempt to develop life goals that are consistent with what we discover.

Finally, having accepted a new source of authority, we commit ourselves to choices and behaviors that are in harmony with our new belief system. When these commitments have been put into practice we should begin to experience the fulfillment of Jesus' life-changing promise. We will know the truth, and applying the truth will set us free from our ineffective patterns of thinking and living.

The truth challenges our personal theology and reveals which parts of our belief systems are faulty. Here are a few "truths" that should affect our approach to living:

1. *We are going to die.* Moses wrote, "Teach us to number our days aright, that we may gain a heart of wisdom" (Ps. 90:12). To "number one's days aright" is to come to grips with the reality that life is short and one day we are going to die. In the Book of Genesis we read that God told Adam the violation of his prohibition would lead to death (Gen. 2:17). The Devil, in the form of a serpent, told Eve that she would not die. This lie, which led to the temptation and fall of humanity, was a denial of death. Pragmatically, many men still live as if this lie were true. It is not. The truth is, you and I are going to die (unless Jesus returns first).

2. *This world is going to pass away and the kingdom of God is coming.* It seems that even those who claim to believe this truth find it difficult to believe it in a way that changes their behavior. The world in which we live is in a state of progressive deterioration. The final destiny of this world is destruction and disintegration. There is a new world coming, a world that is lasting and eternal. You and I can begin to experience a "preview" of the coming kingdom by tapping into the divine blueprint now.

3. *The things of this world will never meet our real needs.* Our motto in this regard should be "Remember Solomon!" Solomon learned that everything the world has to offer produces only frustration, despair, and emptiness. In the chapters that follow I hope to demonstrate that the solution to breaking out of the Solomon Syndrome is found

in a relational network God designed to meet our deepest needs. Only loving relationships, cultivated with a serving attitude and characterized by authentic spirituality, will meet our real needs.

Jesus taught that freedom would be the result of knowing the truth. The truth gives us "magic eyes" that allow us to see life from a different perspective. If we are going to break out of the Solomon Syndrome, we must cultivate perspective. Perspective generates an awareness that enables us to structure our lives with a sense of divinely ordained priority.

Jesus Christ lived a totally free and full life. There was not one trace of bondage in his life. He lived the most satisfying and significant life in all of human history. We often forget that the knowledge, power, and resources to live any way he desired were at his disposal. If those same resources were available to you and me we might have chosen a lifestyle much like Solomon's, but Christ lived a life heavily invested in relationships instead of "stuff." He loved and he served. He lived in harmony with the truth, absolutely free and full of joy. He was perfectly fulfilled. He is our model of what living well really looks like. In order for you and me to live the same way, we probably need to make a few adjustments. Let's begin by seeing how to gain a quality of perspective that motivates us to become unwilling to settle for less in life than God's best!

Personal Reflection

Perhaps you have never given much thought to the idea of manipulated living. Here are a few questions to think about that might help you assess your own life.

1. Do you feel free?
2. How are you trapped in the "rat race"?
3. What is important to you?
4. How does the use of your primary resources reflect the above priorities?
5. Do you want to be liberated?

3

The World According to Tripper Harrison

The Need for Perspective

The word paradigm is often used these days to refer to a person's frame of reference. Stephen R. Covey, who popularized the word in his book, *The Seven Habits of Highly Effective People,* says that a paradigm is "the way we see the world."[1] A paradigm functions as a mental map that provides direction as we travel the road of life. In order for change to occur in our lives it is often necessary to experience what Covey calls a paradigm shift. A paradigm shift requires a change in our philosophy of life. It demands fresh perspective and a new set of priorities to govern our life decisions. To live according to a belief system that goes against the grain of popular culture requires frequent times of appraisal and adjustment. It means a man needs to cultivate a perspective of life that is linked to a set of priorities that enable him to live sanely in what often feels like an insane world.

The challenge men face in this area can be illustrated by a scene from one of my favorite movies, a film called *Meatballs*.[2] The movie is the story of an odd assortment of characters who share a summer together at Camp Northstar. The highlight (or lowlight, depending on how you look at it) of the summer is a weekend of competition that takes place between the young men and women of Camp Northstar and their arch rivals from Camp Mohawk.

To fully appreciate the scene you need to understand something about these two camps. The head counselor of Camp Northstar is a character by the name of Tripper Harrison, played by comedian Bill Murray. It would be an understatement to say that Tripper marches to the beat of a different drummer. Tripper describes Northstar as "the best camping experience available in this price range." Most of the kids who come to spend a summer at Northstar are there because they can't afford to go anywhere else.

Across the lake sits Camp Mohawk, where no expense has been spared in either design or construction. Nor has any expense been spared by the parents of the children who are sent each summer to Camp Mohawk. Every year for the last twelve years the campers of Camp Mohawk have crushed the Camp Northstar campers in the end-of-summer competition.

The scene that grabbed me takes place after the first day of competition in this annual rivalry. Northstar is once again getting creamed. It is evening and the campers from Northstar are sitting around the fireplace, completely dejected. In the midst of their dejection, Tripper stands to speak. His discourse, as I remember it, runs something like this:

"I know what you're thinking," Tripper begins. "For twelve years we've been beaten by these guys. But, you know, it really doesn't matter." The volume of Tripper's voice slowly begins to increase. "They have the best athletes and the best equipment money can buy, but it really doesn't matter." (The campers, still dejected, begin to look up at Tripper.)

"Sure, they have the most sophisticated training programs borrowed from the U.S.S.R. and they have their blood and urine tested daily." (The campers begin to come to life as the volume of Tripper's voice continues to increase.) "But it really doesn't matter!"

"I know they use the latest performance-enhancing drugs, but it really doesn't matter." Tripper is almost shouting. "And even if we were to win, if we were to perform so far over our heads that our noses began to bleed, and if God in heaven were to smile on every man, woman, and child among us, it really doesn't matter!" (The campers are now totally enthralled and on the edge of their seats.) "Because all the really good-looking girls would *still* go out with their guys, because they have all the money! It really doesn't matter!" At this point Tripper begins to lead the entire group as they stand and shout together, "It really doesn't matter! It really doesn't matter! It really doesn't matter!" Of course, as always happens in the movies, with their newfound sense of perspective, the Northstar campers go out the next day and win the competition.

That scene had a rather strange effect on me. For the next few days those words "It really doesn't matter" kept floating through my mind at the most interesting times. I got up in the morning, looked in the mirror at my balding head, and thought, "It really doesn't matter." I sat at a stoplight and someone pulled up next to me in some fine piece of automotive engineering that would normally evoke all manner of covetousness, and a voice inside my head reminded me, "It really doesn't matter!"

The following weekend my wife and I went out to dinner with several couples. One of the women in the group, a fashion consultant, delivered a monologue on the critical importance of what we wear. As I intently maintained the proper communication skills of eye contact mixed with slight affirmative head nod, little could she know that the words floating through my mind were "It really doesn't matter!" Don't get me wrong. All those things (hair, cars, and clothes) are nice. But the fact is that in the big picture of life they really don't matter all that much.

"It really doesn't matter!" Those might be the four most important words in the English language when arranged in that order. They reflect a sense of perspective that is critical if we are to live effectively. Perspective is a critical component of our internal belief system. I believe that every man on the planet (or at least in our culture) is searching for a life that is personally fulfilling and satisfying. I have never met or counseled a man who, at the core of his motivational system, was not engaged in this pursuit. Unfortunately, for many, the pursuit seems as futile as Northstar's attempts to defeat Mohawk. It seems tragic that many men live lives of "quiet desperation" when their hearts long for personal fulfillment. They accomplish little but frustration and despair. For many men one factor producing this futility is the inability to know when to apply these four little words: "It really doesn't matter!"

Failure to achieve fulfillment also involves the "flip side" of these words, that is, the inability to discern and pursue those objectives and goals that really do matter. There is a belief system that will help you answer the question "What really matters?"

At the simplest possible level, the answer is: *You* matter! Your life is important. You were created to live a full and meaningful life. You were created to live with a God-given sense of significance. Your life has a purpose. There is an approach to life that will maximize the joy of living. You really matter!

Not only do you matter, but other people matter. You are surrounded by a network of relationships that were designed to make your life full and meaningful. Relationships really matter. In our frantic pursuit of happiness we often rush by the real sources of joy in life. Men need to understand the design of the universe and how relationships play a central role in that design.

Finally, it is important to know that God really matters. Maybe you don't think of yourself as a religious person; neither do I. Religion is not what really matters. What really matters is a relationship with God that provides us with a spiritual solution to life's challenges. These are the realities that give life meaning and joy. There is a purposeful plan to life that works. Many men have never discovered this truth. When issues of meaning and significance are confronted, they feel a great deal like Arthur Dent.

The Hitchhiker's Guide to the Three-Dimensional Man

How would you feel if you awoke one morning to discover that in exactly twelve minutes the earth was going to be destroyed? Such was the case for Arthur Dent in *The Hitchhiker's Guide to the Galaxy*,[3] the first in a trilogy of books written by Douglas Adams that explores the "big questions" of the meaning of life in a somewhat offbeat manner.

In the trilogy, Arthur Dent and his friend Ford Prefect (who turns out to be a roving reporter for an electronic, cosmic publication called *The Hitchhiker's Guide to the Galaxy*) escape the destruction of our planet by hitching a ride on a passing spaceship called the *Heart of Gold*. During the course of their adventures Arthur discovers that the Earth is actually an artificial planet created to run an organic computer program. In the trilogy, we discover that a race of highly intelligent, pan-dimensional beings designed a computer millions of years ago to answer the question "What is the meaning of life?" "Forty-two" was the computer's answer. The highly intelligent beings were perplexed, to say the least. Upon further inquiry, the computer went on to inform these beings that the answer was meaningless without the right question. Earth was then built to produce "The Question" (if all of this seems a bit bizarre, let me assure you it is! But stick with me for a moment).

At the end of the second book in the trilogy, Arthur and Ford discover "The Question" that fits "The Answer" and theoretically makes sense of life. In a random drawing of letters from a prehistoric word game, the question is formed: "What do you get if you multiply six by nine?" Forty-two? In the BBC production of the trilogy, Arthur comments, "I always knew there was something fundamentally wrong with the universe."

In the final pages of the trilogy it is revealed to Arthur that the question and the answer to the meaning of life are mutually exclusive. Knowledge of one, Arthur is told, logically precludes knowledge of the other. Now, what is the significance of all this insanity? The humorous but tragic message of Mr. Adams's books is that the ultimate meaning of life can never be known. The underlying philosophical presupposition of *The Hitchhiker's Guide to the Galaxy* is that we are all victims of a mass, cosmic, practical joke.

Adams's conclusions are not that uncommon in the world today. Many men in our world feel like they are lost in space. One of the distinctives that sets humanity apart from every other species on the planet is an inborn quest for a sense of meaning and purpose. It is as if our genetic code contains a desire to know what life is all about. We have been designed to live fully only when we are able to discover a sense of meaning and purpose. Without such a sense, men are destined to waste their years either living "lives of quiet desperation" or, more likely, lives of frantic futility. It need not be so. It is possible to know both the question and the answer.

Three-Dimensional Man

There is a divine design in the universe. Your life has a purpose. You can live with a sense of meaning. God has designed a system. When our lives are brought into conformity with this system we will begin to live in a more meaningful and significant way.

To borrow a phrase from the late philosopher and theologian Francis Schaeffer, "He is there, and he is not silent." God is alive, not dead, and he has spoken. There is a divine blueprint for life. The first words of that majestic piece of literature we call the Bible is the statement "In the beginning God created the heavens and the earth" (Gen. 1:1). The God of the Bible is the architect and designer of the world. He created man. In the Bible he has revealed how he designed the cosmos to operate and what has gone wrong with his design. By understanding what "the book" has to say about these things, we will take the first steps toward developing perspective in our lives.

The blueprint is threefold. First, it tells us who we were intended to be. Second, it explains what makes us tick. Third, it describes how we are to live. When you put these three pieces of the puzzle together, you will have "the big picture" of how God designed your life to have meaning and purpose. Each of the next three chapters will deal with one dynamic of this blueprint. It is critical to understand what the Bible has to say about how God designed man.

The Physical Dimension

God is infinite; God is personal. With perfect knowledge, wisdom, power, and love, God chose to create the physical universe. The crowning touch of God's creation was a creature designed to reflect his very image. "God said, 'Let us make man in our image'" (Gen. 1:26). The creation of humanity in the image of God makes it possible for men to live in a meaningful relationship with God himself. Men were created to be three-dimensional beings, living in relationship with the living God.

Many men have been taught that they are nothing more than physical beings. This materialistic view of life leaves little room for any meaningful definition of existence. The materialist's formula for explaining life looks something like this:

TIME + CHANCE + MATTER = LIFE

If you want to know how well this philosophy of life works, take a trip to Russia. For seventy years the people of the former Soviet Union were taught that this formula accurately represented the realities of life on this planet. The results were devastating. Today there is a tremendous spiritual awakening taking place in the Commonwealth countries. Having lived according to the above formula, the people hunger for a spiritual reality to give their lives value and meaning.

In contrast to this definition, the second chapter of the Book of Genesis gives a brief synopsis of human origins from a spiritual perspective. Verse 7 of that chapter affirms the truth that men are physical beings. We read that "God formed the man from the dust of the ground" (Gen. 2:7). However, as the text continues we find that man is much more than a one-dimensional physical being.

As physical beings we are partially composed of matter, fashioned into material bodies which live in contact with the physical world. We experience the physical world through the senses God created. We are able to see, touch, taste, hear, and smell. We have the capacity to experience physical pain and pleasure. These characteristics of our lives are part of the divine design and have been given the divine seal of approval. God said, "It is good!" But you and I are much more than mere physical creatures.

The Psychological Dimension

Genesis 2:7 tells us that God created us to become "living beings." The Hebrew word translated "being" in this passage is often translated to the English word "soul." This is the primary word used in the Old Testament to describe the immaterial part of our being. Along with our physical being, we were designed to be "soulish" creatures. In the New Testament, this part of the nature of men is referred to by use of the Greek word *psyche*. Our English word *psychological* is derived from this Greek word. Man is a psychological being as well as a physical being. The immaterial part of our nature is every bit as important as the material part.

It is our soulish, or psychological, capacities that enable us to think and feel. This part of our nature is often referred to in the Bible as the mind. Mind, when used in this sense, means far more than the physical brain. The mind of man enables him to be a rational and intellectual being like God himself. We think, we feel, and we act because God has created us to be living "beings."

The Spiritual Dimension

In recent years the purely physical view of life has lost many advocates. A two-dimensional view of human nature has become more common. The origins of the personal dimensions of our nature are hotly debated, but at least the psychological part of our being is recognized as fundamental to who we are as men. Now we come to the real watershed of the Genesis passage.

In this brief passage we are told that men are more than psychosomatic beings. The text reveals that God designed man to be three-dimensional. It was the breath of God, imparted to the physical creature, that made man a living soul. The breath of God spoken of in Genesis is a reference to the Spirit of God. The Hebrew words for breath and spirit are used interchangeably in the Old Testament. The Holy Spirit is the third person of what theologians call the Trinity. God designed man to be a physical and emotional being who had the capacity to possess his Spirit. The presence of the Holy Spirit made man a spiritual being who possessed physical, psychological, and spiritual life.

These days you hear the word holistic used in a staggering number of contexts. It is a veritable buzz word among the politically correct. Let me be trendy and political for a minute and say that if we are to live holistically, we must be operating as three-dimensional men. We certainly need to be alive physically and emotionally, but we also need to be functioning spiritually. At the deepest level of our being we need to be in union with God through the work of the Spirit. This three-dimensional nature could be diagrammed as follows:

Three-Dimensional Man

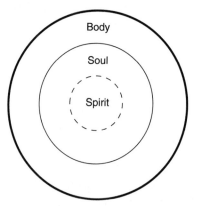

All three dimensions (physical, psychological, and spiritual) are critical. When the spiritual part of man was functioning properly it was intended to influence the operation of the psychological, which in turn would dominate the physical. When all three were in sync, men would be able to live holistically. The logical question is "What went wrong?"

The Lost Dimension

Arthur Dent was right. Something *is* fundamentally wrong with the universe. In the Genesis account we are told that God created man as a three-dimensional being, then placed him in a utopian environment, a beautiful garden called Eden. In this utopian environment the Creator placed one restriction on the man he had created. In the middle of this garden there was a tree called the Tree of the Knowledge of Good and Evil (I guarantee you it was not an apple tree).

God prohibited man from eating from this tree. He was very clear that if his prohibition was violated there would be horrible consequences. Choosing to eat from the restricted tree would constitute an act of moral disobedience, and such disobedience carried with it a death sentence. "When you eat [from the tree] you will surely die," God said (Gen. 2:17).

In the third chapter of the Book of Genesis we read the account of what went wrong. Eve was tempted by the serpent to eat the forbidden fruit. She convinced Adam to do the same. God had told Adam if he ate he would die; the serpent told Eve that they would not die. That was a lie. The serpent convinced Eve that if she and Adam ate the forbidden fruit they would be like God. The issue then was the same issue we face today: Who will be God in our lives? Adam chose to be his own god. The result was death.

If you read the text you might be thinking, "Wait a minute! He didn't die." It is true that upon exercising his freedom to disobey God, Adam did not die physically . . . yet. But something radical took place within his inner being. Before, he had enjoyed an intimate relationship with God; now he was afraid of God. He even hid from God. When confronted, he refused to get honest and instead made excuses for his behavior. His fear of God and the rationalization of his behavior were symptoms of the tragedy that had occurred in his inner being. Adam had died spiritually. Death is the absence of life. The Spirit is the source of spiritual life. The absence of the Spirit produces spiritual death. Adam became two-dimensional. As such he was unable to enjoy the relationship with God he had enjoyed when he was whole.

The spiritual fragmentation of his inner life was reflected in the fact that he blamed Eve for the act of disobedience. Spiritual fragmentation leads to relational fragmentation. Blame and rationalization are usually recognized as signs of internal dysfunction. They are defense mechanisms used to protect damaged emotional systems.

What a dismal picture! In one act of willful disobedience, the first man created disharmony with God, with self, with his spouse, and with his fellowman. You might say that Adam broke ground for the construction of a street called the Boulevard of Broken Dreams.

Spiritual death radically alters the capacity of people to understand and live according to the blueprint God has designed. The very nature of humanity is distorted. When the core of personality is not under the dominant influence of the Spirit of God, the remaining dimensions experience distortion. Apart from God, men seek fulfillment in ways that God never intended, ways that will never meet the deepest needs of the human heart.

Distortion within the spiritual dynamic produces distortion in the emotional system God created. The distortion of these dynamics seriously affects our lives. We get hooked into the Solomon Syndrome. As a result, we live in ways that are dissatisfying and unfulfilling.

But there is a way to get back to three-dimensional living. Albert Einstein once observed that the first step in discovering the solution to a problem is to identify the problem. If you are open to the possibility that the assumptions and observations presented in this chapter have some measure of validity, then you should be encouraged. Having identified the problem, we have the ability to make the adjustments necessary to move our lives back into the sphere of divine intervention and holistic living. Before we undertake that task, let's look at how the loss of the spiritual dimension has affected our psychological systems and the quality of our emotional lives.

Personal Reflection

I hope that what you have just read has created at least some sense of awareness concerning the spiritual dynamic of life. Now is a time to assess your own condition. Take time to read and reflect on the following questions. If you need to make an adjustment, you will find how to do so in the chapters that follow.

1. Have you ever struggled with the meaning of life? Did you find an answer?
2. Have you ever wondered about your own relationship with God?
3. Are you currently living two-dimensionally or three-dimensionally?
4. If God actually had a blueprint for your life, would you like to know what it is?

4

We Are Who We Think Other People Think We Are

An Introduction to Self-Systems Thinking

"How are you?" This is perhaps the most frequently asked question in the human social experience.

"I'm fine. How are you?" This is probably the most frequent response to the most frequently asked question. It is also one of the most frequently told lies, equaled only by the response it asks for, which is usually "Fine." In reality, most men are not fine. They are wounded, insecure, struggling, and don't feel very good about their lives or themselves.

Tim was a struggling pilgrim. For several years he had been attempting to be Christ's man. He faithfully read his Bible. He worked at developing his prayer life. He did a pretty good job of living a life of willing obedience to God. The only thing he struggled with was the most important thing. Tim had a hard time loving people. His marriage was difficult. He felt defeated about the way he treated and sometimes mistreated his children. He had few close friends. Because he had been growing in his relationship with Christ, Tim recognized that his struggle to love was a serious problem. He also began to understand that he didn't love the one person who, along with Christ, he must love in order to authentically love anyone else: Tim didn't love himself.

"How are you feeling?" This was the question Tim was asked early every morning by the psychologist who prescribed a time of isolation and solitude. For twenty-one days Tim lived in a small cabin in the mountains of Colorado. He lived in total isolation. There was no T.V., no radio, no tape player, no books, phone, newspaper—not even a Bible. For twenty-one days he prayed, thought, reflected, and journaled. Tim was alone with himself and God. The experience was called an "intensive," and it is the only appropriate word to describe what those days were like for Tim and for other men who have used this spiritual exercise.

Tim learned many things about himself during those days. He learned how to honestly answer the question "How are you feeling?" He learned that the answer to that question has a great deal to do with the quality of his life. We all long to be able to honestly say "I'm feeling good" when asked that question. Whether we are conscious of it or not, all men want to feel good. We want to feel good about life and we want to feel good about ourselves. Feelings play a central role in the experience of our lives. They are an integral part of our "self system." Our self system is composed of all the internal dynamics of our life that work together to give us a sense of who we are.

Altered States

"Who am I?" "What am I doing here?" "Why am I so confused?" These are the questions that many men find themselves asking. When I first asked these questions in the early sixties I was not in a state of existential angst; I was actually regaining consciousness after being knocked out in a football game. Eventually, I would ask these questions in a more philosophical setting, but in 1964 I wasn't thinking very philosophically. I hadn't started the difficult struggle of defining my identity as a man. Identity, like emotion, is a central dynamic of the self system.

"Who am I?" "What am I doing here?" "Why am I so confused?" This time it was the late sixties. I was a college student, sitting on the floor of a friend's house, listening to the Moody Blues. With my earphones on and the volume cranked up, I was experiencing a significantly altered state of consciousness. Within a matter of months I would begin to discover the answers to those questions. This was the end of my pseudo-hippie phase and I was trying to put life together in a way that made some sense.

"Who am I?" "What am I doing here?" "Why am I so confused?" The year was now 1975. I had been on my spiritual journey for nearly five years. I had been working full-time in the ministry for three years. I had been married for a year and a half. And yet, the answers to these questions were still not crystallized in my thinking. My wife, Allison, and I had taken a few months of sabbatical and moved to Washington, D.C., to live in an intentional community. We were pursuing a work-study program to attempt to get a firm fix on what the next phase of our lives should look like.

It was during these months that I set a personal goal of trying to understand what makes men "tick." I needed to know the answer to the questions I had been asking about my own life, and I wanted to be able to help answer these questions for other men who seemed to be wrestling with the same issues.

During my quest I began to understand what I now consider to be the most important dynamics of human motivation. I discovered that human behavior is motivated by certain needs, what I have previously called *felt* needs, and also what behavioral scientists have labeled *real* needs.

The pioneer of the need-motivated school of psychology was Abraham Maslow. In 1954 Maslow published his book *Motivation and Personality*,[1] in which he postulated his famous hierarchy of needs. Anyone who has ever endured a freshman psychology class has probably been exposed to Maslow's famous hierarchy. The hierarchy is usually diagrammed as a pyramid:

**Maslow's
Hierarchy of Needs**

Self-actualization

Self-esteem

Love and belongingness

Security

Physiological

The theory behind the hierarchy suggests that until our most basic needs are met we are not able to move on to higher levels of growth and fulfillment. A starving man is not usually concerned with his sense of self-esteem. However, once the basic needs are met, a man or woman begins to pursue the higher needs. This drive toward what Maslow called self-actualization, and the needs that must be met to achieve actualization, form the underlying dynamics of the human motivational system according to Maslow's early work.

As illustrated in Maslow's schematic, once our basic physiological and safety needs have been met, the movement toward personal fulfillment passes through the twin needs of love and belongingness. Dr. Larry Crabb, in his book *Effective Biblical Counseling*, uses the terms "security" and "significance" to refer to these same dynamics.[2] The need for security is a need for unconditional love. The need for significance is a need for meaning and purpose. Without a sense of security and a sense of significance we cannot move on to a healthy sense of self-esteem. The longing for a positive sense of self-esteem is the underlying *felt* need that sets the cycle of human motivation into motion. I believe that Crabb, Maslow, and a host of others in the fields of psychology and psychiatry would agree.

In his later years, Maslow recognized that self-actualization was not the highest objective of human development and motivation. He began to talk in terms of self-transcendence, by which he meant that the ultimate objective of life was to live for something greater than ourselves. He was on target.

You and I were not created simply to find our highest fulfillment in becoming self-actualized. If that is our goal, we will cheat ourselves out of the best life has to offer. Solomon was tremendously self-actualized. You and I were actually designed to be "God-actualized." We are not created to simply achieve human potential; we are created to achieve our God-designed potential.

One of the loftiest statements in the history of human literature is the statement that "in the image of God he created him; male and female he created them" (Gen. 1:27). Man was made in the image of God. The theological concept of the image of God has a multitude of implications.

That man exists as a personal being is a reflection of the fact that we are made in the image of God. Human personality, with its intellect, emotions, and power of will, reflects the nature and image of God. The moral dimension of human existence with its sense of "oughtness" (i.e., right and wrong) is an expression of the moral nature of God. You and I were intended to be a reflection of the glory and nature of God. This does not mean, as some have mistakenly assumed, that man is God. Someone once humorously observed that there are two fundamental principles of human enlightenment: #1—*There is a God;* #2—*You are not him!* We are not God, but in many ways we are like God, because God designed us to exist in his image.

Robert Schuller, pastor of the "Crystal Cathedral," teaches that the human drive for self-actualization is simply the reflection of the image of God in man. He calls it "the hunger for glory."[3] I believe he is correct. When we piece together the psychological insights concerning self-esteem with the theology of the image of God we begin to see that our self-concept and how we feel about ourselves is actually a spiritual issue. Self-esteem is "felt" at an emotional level, but it is rooted in a much deeper dimension of our being. Because of the centrality of these issues, it is important to understand how our self-concept is developed.

The Dynamics of Self-Concept

Men are endowed with a unique ability that is both a blessing and a curse. Our intellectual abilities make us capable of being self-conscious. Technically that means that we have the ability to examine our own self and form opinions and feelings about who we are. Those opinions and feelings lie at the heart of the human quest for personal fulfillment.

Self-Image

The human mind goes through a logical process to arrive at the internal mental image we call the "self." The first step in the process involves the construction of an internal mental image of who we are. This internal picture is often called our self-image. Self-image is a highly complex internalized perception. Note the word *perception;* self-image is perceptually based. It may or may not have any objective basis, but is almost entirely subjective.

Chris has lived on a treadmill of repeated failure for many years. One look in his eyes (if you can get him to look you in the eyes) tells you that he is not a happy camper. Everything about your first encounter with Chris would lead you to label him a "loser." What you can't see by looking at Chris is how he came to be the way he is.

Chris believes he is a loser. It is a primary component of his self-image. It was a message he heard from his earliest childhood. Abandoned at birth, Chris spent his early years in a string of abusive foster homes. The abuse was never blatant; social services made sure physical abuse was not tolerated. Emotional abuse is more difficult to detect. In Chris's case it was primarily a function of neglect.

Chris was born with special needs. Had he been raised in the proper environment, his learning disabilities might have been detected early. If he had parents who cared, special help could have been found to help him learn to succeed in school. His life, in all probability, would have turned out quite different. Instead, Chris failed. His teachers and foster parents formed the opinion that Chris was stupid. This opinion was communicated consistently to Chris by every look they gave and every word they spoke. Chris came to believe that he was stupid and that he would always be a loser. This conviction lies at the heart of Chris's self-image. His life has been one long self-fulfilling prophecy flowing from this perception.

Ironically, and tragically, Chris is actually quite intelligent. When his intelligence was finally tested, he scored in the superior range. Unfortunately, Chris is convinced the tests were wrong. His perception is stronger than the hard data.

Internally, it is our perception that is real to us. For instance, one of the more common eating disorders our culture has spawned is called *anorexia nervosa*. One component of this very complicated disorder is the perception that one is obese. Most people who suffer from this disorder eventually have the appearance of a concentration camp survivor. Yet when they look in the mirror they see a "fat" person. Perception forms their "reality," even though their perception has no basis in objective fact. It is critical to understand that self-concept is much like this eating disorder. It is an internal perception that does not necessarily have a basis in objective reality.

Another critical dimension of self-concept we see demonstrated in Chris's case is the fact that it is developed primarily through reflected appraisal. Our self-concept is the product of what we think others think about us. Again, our appraisal might be horribly skewed. Dr. Vernon Grounds, President Emeritus of Denver Seminary, has observed, "We are not who we think we are; and we are not

who others think we are. We are who we think others think
we are."

The self-image is an internal picture of what we perceive
to be our strengths, weaknesses, adequacies, attractive-
ness, intelligence, goodness, value, and lovability. Our
mind, in all its warped and wonderful complexity, puts all
this perceived data together and forms this internal image
we call the self.

Self-Worth

Self-image breaks down into further subcategories based
on what our mind does with this internal perceived image.
Having formed an internal picture of who we are, our mind
also forms an image of who we think we should be. Somewhere in our inner being is a reservoir of all the "shoulds,"
"oughts," "dos," "don'ts," "goods," and "bads" of a lifetime. Freud called this component of the psyche the super-
ego. David Seamands refers to this factor of our internal
landscape as "Super You."[4] Again, as a product of perception and reflected appraisal, you and I have this internalized image of who we think we should be. Here comes the
kicker! Along with the capability the brain possesses to
form these two internal images, it has the ability to compare the two and evaluate the inevitable discrepancy between the perceived self (who we think we are) and the
ideal self (who we think we *should* be).

Once we begin to compare our image of who we think
we are with our image of who we think we should be, we
begin to place a sense of value on our self. This attach-
ment of value to our self-image produces our sense of self-
worth.

Dan feels worthless. Not many people know how Dan
feels; he covers it well with bravado. This feeling of worth-

lessness has been a constant source of relational difficulties in Dan's life.

The reasons Dan feels worthless are complex. To simplify, Dan has an unrealistic internal image of who he should be. This image is a product, primarily, of neurotic parenting within a dysfunctional family. Unrealistic goals and expectations were "programmed" into Dan at a very early age. His mental "tape recorder" is filled with "shoulds" and "oughts" and "why didn't yous." When Dan compares his perceived self with his ideal self, he always falls short. Dan needs some help unraveling this problem.

Self-worth is that part of the self-concept that bridges the gap between the cognitive (or thinking) area and the affective (or feeling) dimension of self-concept. Our sense of self-worth places a heartfelt evaluation on who we are. Our evaluation will either be positive, generating a sense of value and worth, or, like Chris and Dan, the evaluation will be negative, creating a sense of personal unworthiness or worthlessness. For most of us, this evaluation is something of a mixed bag. Isn't the mind a wonderful thing?

Self-Esteem

One final process in the mind's formation of the self-concept remains to be mentioned. First, having formed a perceived internal image of who we think we are and who we think we should be, then having evaluated the discrepancy between the two and having attached a perceived value to our person, some bizarre part of the brain then attaches a feeling component to the whole package. If life (and our mom and dad) has been kind, we might be among the lucky carbon-based life-forms on the planet who actually feel good enough about them-

selves to move toward living out their full God-given potential. If, on the other hand, the experiences of life have
been less than kind, and if we have had the bad fortune of growing up in a less than functional or a non-
nurturing home, chances are that our self-esteem will be
low and our emotional life will be something of a struggle. We will not feel good about ourselves. Since this factor is so powerful, many men go through life engaging
in some of the most bizarre enterprises imaginable in
order to feel good about themselves. This is not how the
system was designed.

This component of our inner world is perhaps the single most significant motivating dynamic of life. The need
for a positive sense of self-esteem will unconsciously drive
much of our behavior. How we seek to get this need met
will depend on the second factor in the cycle of human
motivation. All of us carry around certain basic assumptions about life inside our heads and hearts. These assumptions constitute our belief system. This belief system
dictates how we seek to meet the need for self-esteem. Remember Norma Jean?

There are only two options concerning the source of
our personal belief systems. One is humanistic; the other
is spiritually-based. Most of us spend a great many years
pursuing the humanistic options. When they fail to meet
the deepest needs of our lives we hopefully might begin
to seek something that transcends humanistic theories.
This pursuit will eventually lead us to seek spiritual answers to the questions we ask. We begin to question
whether or not there might not be a divine design for living. We might even begin to wonder if God has designed
a way to live that will fully meet these deep needs. Many
men have discovered that there is an affirmative answer
to these questions. This discovery often reveals that our
basic assumptions about how to get our needs met are
not consistent with the "blueprint" we discover. At that

point we will have a very important decision to make. Are we going to live our lives on the basis of faulty assumptions, or are we willing to live consistently with what God has designed to meet our needs and move us toward full actualization and on to transcendence? The answer to that question will shape the course of our lives. Coming to terms with these issues requires some time of reflection and assessment.

At the heart of how we feel about ourselves is our experience of love. We often think that only women need to have an experience of love to meet their needs; this is a faulty assumption. God also created men with the need for unconditional love. Our need for love exceeds the human capability to give love. If we are going to feel good about ourselves we will need to tap into a source of overpowering love. Such a source exists. This realization takes place as we take the time to stop and assess "How am I really feeling?" and as we ask the tough question "Is the course of my life leading me into the sources that will meet my real needs?" Such a course exists. It is found in prioritizing a network of relationships God designed to meet our deepest needs. How we interact with this network will make all the difference in the quality of our existence and how we feel about life and ourselves.

Personal Reflection

Before moving on, take a few minutes to reflect on what you've read in this chapter. Here are a few questions you might ask yourself:

1. Do you have a conscious understanding of your needs?

2. At what level on Maslow's hierarchy do you see yourself?
3. How do you feel about yourself?
4. Do you consider yourself a valuable person?
5. Is your belief system working to meet your deepest needs?

5

Buckets, Ladders, and Paradigm Shifts

Understanding the Relational Network

A t age thirty-seven Jim came to realize that a spiritual solution existed that addressed life's challenges. Through a group of friends he came to understand what it meant to have a personal relationship with Jesus Christ. Jim gave his life to Christ and began growing spiritually. As his relationship with Christ matured, Jim found himself forced to make a decision that would forever alter the course of his life. He had to decide whether he would seek to discover and live a life based on God's design or whether he would continue to live according to the chaotic plan he had been following for years. Jim was wrestling with his belief system.

Thinking through this decision, Jim had the good fortune of having one of those rare moments of clarity that seem to come all too infrequently in life. He thought, "If this is true, what could be more important than discovering God's plan?" Not too profound, I guess, but for Jim it was just that simple.

For the next few years Jim studied great amounts of data relating to the whole subject of God's plan. For the first time ever he began to read the Bible. He had picked the book up once or twice before but never seemed able to make any sense out of it. He always seemed to turn to some long and obscure genealogy that seemed completely irrelevant to the real issues of life. Now, with a new commitment to discovering a spiritually-based plan for his life, the book came alive.

Jim also devoured a great number of books on a wide variety of subjects relating to spiritual issues. It seemed that the more he read and studied, the more there was for him to understand. Jim began to feel that perhaps God's plan was so complex that it would take a lifetime to figure out.

At about the same time in his spiritual journey, Jim was exposed to a relatively simple framework that tied together the vast amount of data his brain had accumulated. At a men's Bible study he heard his pastor teach on the subject of relational priorities. The message was based on an incident that occurred in the life of Christ.

One day Jesus was asked what is surely the best question anyone ever asked a man who claimed to be the Son of God. Matthew relates that an expert in the Law tested Jesus with this question: "Teacher, which is the greatest commandment in the Law?" (Matt. 22:36). As Jim listened to his pastor he found himself wondering if the motivation for this question might have been the same frustration he was experiencing. After all, think about all the data this "expert" had accumulated over the years. Dr. Bob told the men to think of the question as being paraphrased like this: "If you take all the information in this big book and boil it down to its essence, is there any unifying principle that ties it all together?" This was the question Jim had been asking himself for several years.

Jesus told the scribe (the meaning of the NIV phrase translated "expert in the law") that the first and greatest commandment was to "Love the Lord your God with all your heart and with all your soul and with all your mind" (Matt. 22:37–38). He continued by adding that there was a second command of like significance: "Love your neighbor as yourself" (Matt. 22:39). Bob told the men that the purpose of life, according to Jesus Christ, is to love God and to love each other. Loving relationships are at the heart of the divine design for life. Suddenly, Jim knew that what he had been looking for was amazingly simple. He needed to learn what it meant to love God and his neighbor.

Back to the Garden

If we go back to the creation account of Genesis and look at it through the filter of Jesus' statements, we can see how God developed a perfect system in which all of our needs for love and meaning were intended to be met in an amazing network of relationships.

We have already seen how the second chapter of Genesis gives us a picture and explanation of who we were intended to be. We were designed by God to be three-dimensional men: body, soul, and spirit. We have also made note of the mind-boggling truth that as three-dimensional beings we were to exist in the very image or reflection of our Creator. Now, as we read on in this second chapter of Genesis we will discover a strategy for how we were intended to live.

Having created man, God designed and developed a utopian environment in which he placed Adam. Living in relationship with the living God and experiencing what seems to be very clear communication with him, Adam was also assigned the task of working in this environment to take care of it. When we reach the eighteenth verse of this chapter we read what is perhaps one of the most significant statements in all of the Bible.

Up until this point, every act of God and every product of his creative exercise had been evaluated by God as "good." Five times in the first chapter of Genesis we read the phrase "and God saw that it was good." Finally, after the creation of man, God appraised all that he had made and said that "it was *very* good" (Gen. 1:31, italics mine). When we get to the eighteenth verse of the second chapter, we read for the first time that something about creation was found to be problematic. God said, "It is not good for the man to be alone." In response to this evaluation, God put Adam to sleep and created Eve; interpersonal relationships were born. God then personally presided over the first wedding, and the covenant of marriage was established. With marriage came the possibility for the creation of families. As families grew, an intermarried community could develop. In these short verses we see the raw material for living according to a set of divinely ordained priorities. Let's put it together.

First, God provided a primary and secondary channel for meeting man's need for love. The primary channel for meeting this need was to be a man's personal relationship with God himself. You were created to live in loving relationship with God. The critical word here is relationship. God is not *primarily* interested in what we believe or don't believe. God is not *primarily* interested in what we do or don't do. God is *primarily* interested in *us*. He created us to live in a love relationship with himself. What God desires is to love us and have us receive and respond to his love with our love. This is why Jesus had to remind the experts that the heart of the issue was to "love God with all your heart." The central message of the Bible is "Love God and let God love you!"

Many men have a difficult time making the mental transition from viewing God as a demanding tyrant or celestial policeman to understanding that he is a loving Father. This transition is the pivotal internal change that will begin to move us toward a life that is consistent with the spiritual blueprint. Without an experience of the unconditional love of God, we will never fully have our need for love or security met. Regardless of how rich our interpersonal relationships are, they are never perfectly unconditional. Only God can love us unconditionally. The ultimate expression of God's unconditional love was the gift of his Son, Jesus. In the life and death of Jesus we are able to see and experience perfect unconditional love. Through a relationship with Jesus Christ we are able to experience spiritual life and fellowship with God. This relationship becomes the foundation for living according to the divine blueprint. It also forms the first rung on a conceptual ladder that will help you understand how the network of relationships God has established fits together.

The Ladder of Love

The network of relationships God designed to meet our needs contains a sequence of priorities. Jesus clearly told the scribe that the first and greatest commandment was to love God with our whole being (Matt. 22:37). He then went on to say that a second command was like it: "Love your neighbor as yourself" (Matt. 22:38). The word "neighbor" encompasses all human relationships.

Within this broad category is a biblical sequence of priority. If you are married, your husband or wife is your "neighbor." If you have children, your sons and daughters are your "neighbors." If you are part of a church, your spiritual brothers and sisters are your "neighbors." Your real-life neighbors are also your "neighbors," and the person who works at the filling station where you buy gas is your "neighbor." As a matter of fact, even people on the other side of the planet, living in cultures radically different from your own, are your "neighbors."

Each of these categories of "neighbor" fits within a system of priorities mapped out for us in the Bible. Visually and conceptually, this system of priorities can be illustrated by using the image of a ladder. Each rung on the ladder represents a category of relationships set in its proper priority. This tool can serve as a mental filter through which we view the world and with which we are able to prioritize how we are going to live our lives.

Ladder of Love
The Relational Paradigm

1. God

2. Self

3. Wife

4. Kids

5. Friends

6. Fellowman

Priority #1

The top rung of the ladder represents the highest priority relationship of life. Above and beyond all the factors that contribute to living consistently in the will of God, our direct, immediate, and personal relationship with God is to hold the preeminent place. This relationship is not only the top priority in the network, it is also the primary channel through which our security or love need is to be met. God is ready, willing, and able to love us unconditionally. He designed the system and he is able to meet the need.

This relationship with God is also critical in getting our need for significance met. Only when we are in the proper relationship with God can we fully understand and enter into the channels through which we gain the sense of significance that moves our lives toward our full potential.

Our primary source of significance is to be found in the truth that we are created in the image of God. We were intended and designed to be reflectors of the divine image. The framers of the *Westminster Confession of Faith* expressed this truth by stating that the chief aim or purpose of man is to glorify God and enjoy him forever.[1] Our being and existence is to be the primary source of our significance. Many biblical images of purpose support this conviction. Jesus said we are to be salt and light in the world (Matt. 5:13–14). Salt and light obviously have tasks to perform that fall into the category of "doing," but it is the very nature of salt and light that enable them to perform these tasks. Therefore, "if the salt loses its saltiness" it is no longer good for accomplishing its task. Salt must *be* salt!

In the New Testament, the apostle Paul writes about the experience of Moses when he received the law of God. Having been in the presence of God, Moses came down the mountain reflecting and radiating the glory of God. Paul draws the conclusion that the purpose of our existence is to reflect the Lord's glory, like Moses, as we are transformed into his image (2 Cor. 3:18). By our very being we are to reflect the glory of God. Obviously, something has gone wrong. But remember, we are exploring the original intentions of God and the systems he designed to enable men to live meaningfully and significantly.

Every human being is of eternal significance to God because every human being, however flawed and imperfect, bears something of the divine image. Every man or woman living on the planet, simply by virtue of his or her existence, is significant. As one small child observed, "God made me and he doesn't make any junk!" Only in the proper relationship with God do these realities begin to come into focus and affect our experience. Ultimately, our self systems are dependent upon spiritual realities.

Along with these lofty callings to be image bearers and to live in relationship with God, secondary channels for meeting both the need for security and the need for significance were put in place in this relational network.

Priority #2

When Jesus stated that the purpose of life was to love God and one another he added a qualifying statement. Jesus said we should love our neighbor as ourselves (Matt. 22:39). The question has been repeatedly raised in both theological and psychological circles whether it is even possible to love one's neighbor without a healthy sense of self-love. Previously I attempted to develop a brief overview of the dynamics of the self system. Let me add one further dimension to the matrix of self-image, self-worth, and self-esteem. Self-love is the fourth logical component of the self system.

When exploring the concept of self-love a fundamental decision must be made. With what content do you load the word "love"? If love is given a cultural definition, self-love becomes self-centered and narcissistic. Self-love defined egocentrically becomes unhealthy and destructive. Since the entire biblical frame of reference negates self-centeredness, loving one's self must be defined differently. When love is given its proper definition, self-love is perfectly consistent with God's plans and purpose.

When Jesus spoke to the scribe about loving, he used the Greek word *agape*. This kind of love seeks the highest welfare of the object loved. It is an action-oriented word that requires an act of the will. If the object loved is yourself, then to love yourself means to seek your own highest welfare. Since the will of God for our lives is the best life possible, if we truly love ourselves with *agape* love we will seek God's will. This is the definition of self-love that permeates the divine blueprint.

God's will for our lives calls us to deny ourselves. We are instructed to say "no" to self-will and "yes" to God's will. In doing so we learn to die to self. At first glance it might look like a contradiction in terms when the Bible tells us to both love ourselves and deny ourselves. Actually, these two commands perfectly complement one another.

In one of the most complex statements Jesus made, he told his followers that whoever tried to save his life would lose it, but whoever lost his life for Jesus' sake would find it (Luke 9:24). The irony of the self relationship is that it is the one relationship in the relational paradigm whose needs can never be met by concentrating directly on them. The needs of the self are actually met in the process of dying to self and investing in and concentrating on the other priority relationships of the paradigm.

I often think of this paradox by using the image of a series of buckets that need to be filled. The more we try to fill the self bucket, the emptier it gets. Finally, when we give up on filling the self bucket and begin to concentrate on the other buckets (God, marriage, family, friends, and fellowman), guess what happens? While filling the other buckets the self bucket has been mysteriously filled; it was in losing our life (self) that we found our life (self). This is the beauty and irony of the self relationship. To love yourself (that is, seek God's best for yourself), concentrate on the other priorities of the ladder.

Priority #3

When God made the statement "it is not good for man to be alone," he had already entered into a relationship with Adam. The primary channel for meeting humanity's need for love was in place. God then designed a series of human relationships to serve as the secondary channels for meeting that need. The man was put to sleep and a part of his being was removed and fashioned into a woman. From one came two, who were brought back together to become one. The marriage relationship was designed and instituted. For those of us who are married, this relationship is intended to be our highest priority after our relationship with Christ. As men, we are actually commanded to love our wives like Christ loves the church (Eph. 5:25).

If you are single you face two exciting possibilities. It is possible that some day you will be married. At that point your marriage will become a major priority. On the other hand, God's plan for your life might be for you to stay single. In that case God himself will occupy this space in a special way. It is clear in the Bible that Jesus was single. The Father's plans for his earthly life required that Jesus not have a physical wife and family.

The apostle Paul was most likely also single. It is possible that at one time he was married, but by the time he wrote his letters he was single. God's plan for his life also necessitated that he remained single. I think it would be safe to say that both Jesus and Paul, along with many men throughout the ages, have lived full and meaningful lives without being married. Biblically, both marriage and singleness are viewed as special callings from God. For those of us who have the calling to married life, our spouse is to be our highest earthly priority; for those who are called to be single, relationships with friends and fellowman assume a higher priority.

Priority #4

The next rung on the ladder represents our relationships with our children. For those of us who are fathers, our children are to be our highest priority after our wives. When God designed the marriage relationship, he designed humans with the capacity to "be fruitful and increase in number" (Gen. 1:28). God created families as a secondary channel to meet our needs for love and significance. The family was intended to form the nucleus of God's design for the human community. Our children are a vital part of God's system of priorities. Learning to make our children the priority God intended them to be is not only important, it is one of the great sources of joy and fulfillment in life.

Priority #5

As families grew and multiplied, human community was created. I believe God intended the world to be filled with communities of people that love and serve him and one another. These communities provide increased opportunities for relationships. In the midst of the community, we need a few close friendships to help us be the men God intended us to be. We need each other. In our fast-paced, technological world, community does not come naturally. If we are to experience what the Bible calls fellowship, it will take determination on our part. Making our relationships with a small number of other men a priority is a major component of the blueprint, and another important factor in getting our needs for love and meaning met.

Priority #6

The final rung of the ladder is entitled "Fellowman." This is an extremely comprehensive term. It is also a critically important term. By acknowledging this rung on the ladder, we are making a statement about the value of all people and the priority of relationships over productivity or accumulation.

In our culture we are constantly bombarded with the false message that living well hinges on the accumulation of "stuff." Many people go through life with the often unconscious philosophy of "love things, use people." The fellowman rung will require a change in our thinking. It requires a commitment to a new philosophy of "love people, use things," of finding significance through the secondary channel of serving people.

These six areas of relationship (God, self, marriage, family, friends, and fellowman) form a relational network. They constitute a framework of priorities designed by God to make life full and meaningful. The choice to make these relationships the priorities of our lives constitutes a radical paradigm shift. Our convictions about these issues inform and redefine our belief system. The goals we set and the actions we take to meet these goals transform our lifestyles. Life viewed through this filter and lived according to these priorities looks radically different from life lived in conformity to the mold of culture.

Every decision you make has implications for some relationship on the ladder. If you have a major decision to make you can evaluate the decision on the basis of how this decision will affect your relationship with God. Will the change enhance or detract from your ability to love and serve God? Is the change motivated by an egocentric desire to inflate your own sense of self-esteem and meet your own ego needs? Does the change have any negative impact on the time and energy you will have available to cultivate your relationships with your wife and children?

The ladder is of equal value in making a decision as simple as responding to an invitation to play golf on Saturday. If the invitation comes from a friend whose relationship is a priority on the ladder you will have a strong tendency to make an affirmative decision. But before you say "yes," you need to decide whether spending the day with your wife and children is what you really need to be doing on Saturday. The beauty of having a tool like this lies in the fact that if you have already been concentrating on these priorities daily, your relationship with your family might already have received adequate time and energy. You will then be free to enjoy that occasional Saturday on the golf course without guilt or remorse.

This ladder of relational priorities is a tool you can use to assess where your life is heading. If the actual priorities of your life are out of alignment with this relational filter, then you know it is time for some adjustment. As we move on through this book I will make some suggestions about how to accomplish that task.

To the extent that your life is built on a commitment to making these relationships the priorities of your life, you will be well on the way to living a life of substance and significance. To the extent that you are structuring your life on a set of priorities shaped by some other factor, you will probably find that you are heading down a Boulevard of Broken Dreams, well on the way to a life of disillusionment, frustration, and even despair.

In the second part of this book I am going to walk you through each relationship in the network. Before I do, however, it would be helpful to look at a few steps that need to be taken at this point to break out of the Solomon Syndrome and make the following chapters most helpful.

Personal Reflection

If the ideas presented in this chapter are new to you, it might be helpful to spend a few minutes reflecting before moving on. Here are a few questions related to this chapter to use in your time of assessment:

1. Do you understand the concept of a relationship with God?
2. Who are the people God has placed in your relational paradigm?
3. What are the top priorities of your life as reflected by your use of time, money, and energy?
4. Is there anything in the way you are living that you would like to change?

6

Exit This Way

Four Steps to Make the Break

Nearly twenty years ago Bill was running down the Boulevard of Broken Dreams at full speed. He had spent years building a successful business as a manufacturer's representative for a computer company. He had also spent years neglecting his wife and children while developing a tidy package of very bad habits. He drank too much, smoked too much, dabbled in drug use, and chased other women. One night Bill had an experience for which he will be eternally grateful. Bill pulled over, out of the fast lane, and paused long enough to take a look at where he was heading. What he observed was so distressing that it changed the course of his life.

Bill saw that the world was in trouble! He thought about what life must have been like before there were cars, trucks, roads, and buildings. He thought about the raw material of life on the planet and the potential that once existed for the development of a civilized world. Then Bill compared the potential with what actually existed.

He seemed to see life through a different set of lenses that night. He was beginning to experience a paradigm shift. Everything looked warped and distorted. He watched rusted and dented cars roll down cracked and potholed streets, and the cars appeared to be occupied by very unhappy people who seemed to be in a great hurry to get nowhere.

Bill looked at the landscape and saw chaotically designed houses and buildings in a state of disrepair and disintegration. There was no evidence of the beauty of nature. The buildings appeared to be filled with men who spent much of their days doing unfulfilling work in order to buy things they didn't need and that would never make them happy. It was a very bleak set of images.

But the bleakness of that picture was nothing compared to what Bill saw when he looked within. He saw himself in those cars, houses, and office buildings. He began to realize that he had no idea what life was about. At first this was a horribly depressing experience; he realized that he was heading nowhere fast. In a state of near despair, he realized that he didn't know how to change his course or whether there was a way of life that made sense.

Fortunately (or I should say graciously), he made two critical decisions that night. First, Bill put the brakes on his life. He simply stopped running down the road. He was no longer willing to accept the status quo and continue to pursue a meaningless life simply because it was the norm. Second, Bill made a decision to attempt to discover if life had meaning and purpose. He wanted to know if there was a way of life that was meaningful and significant. Without much of a spiritual background, he decided that he needed to know if there was a God and what he was like.

Bill discovered that life doesn't need to be chaotic and meaningless. He found an approach to living that has been proven solid and substantive to him for over twenty years. The preceding chapters of this book contain much of what Bill began to discover that night. Bill is one of the lucky few who came to realize that he needed to make a break from the Solomon Syndrome. Let me walk you through the decisions Bill made to make that break.

Decision One: Becoming Three-Dimensional

To break away from the Solomon Syndrome and begin to develop a life structure consistent with the divine blueprint, we must first make sure that we are three-dimensional men. We have seen that the intention of God is for us to be spiritual beings. But by nature we are not.

Every man on the planet is born dead. We are alive physically, but dead spiritually. Understanding this fact will help us understand why Jesus told a man named Nicodemus that the missing ingredient in his quest for the kingdom of God was a second birth experience (John 3:3). Nicodemus had been born physically, but he had never experienced spiritual birth. What was true of Nicodemus is also true of you and me.

One of the clearer images explaining how to become three-dimensional again is found in the New Testament Book of Revelation. In the third chapter of this book Jesus Christ paints a word picture of what needs to happen in each of our lives if we are to become spiritual men. Jesus says, "Here I am! I stand at the door and knock" (Rev. 3:20). The door Jesus is referring to is a symbolic door; you might imagine it as the door to your heart or inner being. Jesus is knocking on this door because he wants to enter our lives and give us spiritual life. He goes on to tell us what must happen in order for us to experience spiritual birth: "If anyone hears my voice and opens the door, I will come in" (Rev. 3:20).

We must respond to Christ by making a decision to personally invite him to invade our lives. When we do, he will come to dwell in our innermost being by means of the person of the Holy Spirit. When the Spirit comes, he

Three-Dimensional Man

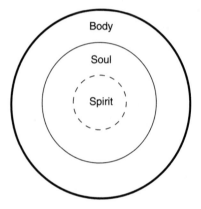

imparts spiritual life to us. His very presence in our inner being makes us three-dimensional once again.

When Bill reached the point in his life where he knew something needed to change, he decided to visit a church attended by several of his coworkers. One of these men had very tactfully and sensitively communicated to Bill that he would always be welcome there. When the time came, Bill knew where to go.

That morning the minister explained how to make this decision. Bill sensed that God had orchestrated the message just for him. At the end of the message, the minister invited anyone who had never asked Christ into his or her life to pray this prayer with him:

Lord Jesus, I need you. Thank you for dying on the cross for me. I want to turn from my self-centered and self-directed life and follow you. Come into my life, Lord Jesus. I open the door and receive you as Savior and Lord. I want to be the kind of man or woman you want me to be. I want to live according to your divine blueprint.

Bill prayed this prayer with sincerity of heart. By doing so he took the first step in the adjustment process. His life has never been the same. If you have never made this decision, now is the time to do so. Read the words of the prayer Bill prayed. Do they express the desire of your heart? If so, bow your head and pray the same prayer.

Decision Two: Affirming Your Real Needs

By inviting Jesus Christ into our lives we take the first step toward developing a relationship with the living God. We are then enabled to begin to see life from God's point of view as we come alive spiritually. This in turn will help each of us answer the critical question "What do I really need?"

Bill didn't realize that by receiving the new life Christ gives, he actually met the greatest *real* need in his life. As he began to grow spiritually, his understanding of his other needs also began to fall into place. Bill came to understand that all men, himself included, have the twin needs of unconditional love and meaning. By identifying and embracing these two needs as the most important needs of his emotional life, Bill made the second decision in the process of life structuring. Only as we identify and affirm our real needs are we able to begin to develop a belief system that is in harmony with the relational paradigm. If we plug these two factors into our schematic of human motivation it looks like this:

Dynamics of Human Motivation

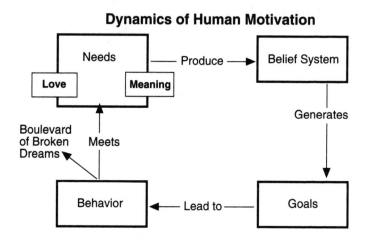

Decision One changes our entire perspective of the nature of life. Decision Two clearly identifies the first components of the human motivation system. We are now ready to move to the critical third decision in the adjustment process.

Decision Three: Redefining Your Belief System

Bill began to make choices about how he was going to get his real needs met. Bill wanted to develop a belief system that was filled with a commitment to God's plan for his life. He wanted to replace his "bad theology and geometry" with the truth. Bill began making the third decision.

How are you going to live? How are you going to invest your time, energy, and resources? At this point you will want to plug the relational network of the ladder of love into your personal philosophy of life. This decision further refines our motivational schematic to look like this:

Dynamics of Human Motivation

In a biblically based life structure, our relationship with Christ is to be our highest priority. We need to take the time, exert the energy, and invest the resources necessary to develop our spiritual lives. We must determine that we will heavily invest our primary resources in this divinely ordained network of relationships. When this network becomes intimately integrated into our belief system, we are ready to make the fourth decision.

Decision Four: Building Priority Relationships

The fourth decision requires action. Bill's new belief system led him to make some choices and institute some new behaviors that reflected his new philosophy of life. If we have adopted the conceptual elements of the divine blueprint, Decision Four will require actions that develop this network of relationships.

Two key words permeated Bill's process of setting new goals that were consistent with his new priorities. The first word was *love*. Bill recognized that it was his job to implement behaviors that would build loving relationships on every rung of the ladder. Love is an action word. Bill recognized that he needed to invest time and energy in these relationships to genuinely know and authentically care for the people God had placed in his life.

The second key word for Bill was *serve*. Love always leads to service. Bill began to shift the focus in his relationships in order to reach out and care for the people in his network. He began to discover that his commitment to serve affected his own need for personal significance. Bill began to feel that his life was really counting for something important.

What will all this look like for you? It probably will look a little different for each of us. In the second part of this book I am going to take each rung on the ladder and help you see what making these relationships a priority might look like. I also hope to give you some ideas on how to cultivate these relationships in your own life.

If you make these four decisions—(1) become a three-dimensional man, (2) identify and affirm your real needs, (3) develop a spiritually based belief system, and (4) begin to build priority relationships—I can promise you this: You will be able to break out of the Solomon Syndrome. In a very real sense you will take the exit off the Boulevard of Broken Dreams marked "True Security and Real Significance." You will head down a road that will lead to a life of meaning, satisfaction, and personal fulfillment. You will start to live in a way that reaps the benefits of living according to God's divine blueprint.

Personal Reflection

You are now at a critical juncture in this book. In the next chapters you will have the opportunity to look at each major area of relationship in your life. Before you move on, use this time to honestly assess your life. Reflect on the following questions:

1. To what degree does your life feel manipulated or intentional?
2. How well does your use of time, energy, and money align with what you say are your priorities?
3. Carefully look at each of the four decisions in this chapter. Have you made each one?

Part Two

Bridges, Networks, and Promises Kept

A Tool for Adjustment

7

Making Love Last

What Solomon Never Found Out

The scenario is repeated on numerous occasions. A boy and girl meet, fall in love, and make that monumental decision to get married. The date is set, arrangements are made, tuxedos are rented, and invitations are sent. Finally, the big day arrives. In the presence of friends and family, the boy and girl look into each other's eyes and say those magic words, "I do." The guests throw rice, the couple jumps in the getaway car, and they live happily ever after. Wouldn't it be great if that was the way it always worked?

Unfortunately, all too often the smiling faces of the wedding day turn into the disappointed and angry faces of the attorney's office. It should not be that way. In his somewhat offbeat love story, *Still Life with the Woodpecker*, Tom Robbins observes that the great question in the last quarter of the twentieth century is "How do you make love last?"[1] This is an immensely significant observation.

Every day I hear of another marriage that has ended in divorce. As I pick my son up from school, I see children on their way home to spend the rest of the evening without either a mom or a dad. In one nearby high school, 80 percent of the students live in single-parent homes. Why do so many marriages fail? I believe it is because we have not learned how to answer the question "How do you make love last?"

My wife and I know the pain of this struggle. There was a time in our own marriage when we both wondered whether or not we were going to make it. By the grace of God, and with the help of a few good friends (some of whom we paid at the rate of seventy-five dollars an hour), we worked hard to find the answer to that question. Our commitment to the principles contained in the first part of this book made the difference between becoming another divorce statistic and molding our marriage into a healthy and vital relationship. Let me share with you what we learned about how to make love last.

The Great American Myth

The problems that lead to the loss of love begin with the tremendous misunderstanding in our culture about the nature of real love. Take a second to think of all the different contexts in which this word *love* is used. I *love* my wife; I *love* my kids; I *love* my dog; I still *love* the Beatles; and sometimes I even *love* my car. The word *love* has become almost meaningless because we fail to distinguish between the different states of mind and emotion to which we attach this little four-letter word.

If you want a solid definition of love as it relates to marriage, you need to go back to the divine blueprint. In

Greek, the language of the New Testament, a variety of words were used to communicate the series of ideas for which we use the word *love*. Three of these words must be combined to develop a holistic understanding of real love.

Eros

The first of those Greek words is *eros*, from which our English word *erotic* is derived. This word was used to express the physical attraction that occurs between a man and a woman. Love has a physical dimension. Much of the American myth of love is rooted in the sensual or sexual dimension of love.

God is the author and creator of this dimension of love. In the proper context, sexuality is not only important, it is good. As a matter of fact, in the proper context it is great! God designed us to be male and female. He built into the very fabric of our beings the biological drives that attract us to the opposite sex. Those of us who are already married would probably have to honestly admit that our initial attraction to our mates was not based on some deep spiritual quality we discerned in our beloved; we simply liked the way he or she looked and felt a strange biochemical process stirring within.

Eros does have its problems, though. It is an inadequate type of love on which to build a lasting relationship. If this is the only dimension of love present in a relationship, the relationship will be shallow and one-dimensional. *Eros* comes and *eros* goes. *Eros* is fickle and fading. *Eros* by itself can also get us into a lot of trouble. Some days I just won't feel this kind of love for my mate. This lack of attraction is enough of a problem by itself, but it is compounded when I don't feel *eros* for my mate—but I do feel it for someone else's mate. In such cases, *eros* can lead to a problem the Bible calls adultery.

C. S. Lewis referred to *eros* as the "I love you if . . ." kind
of love. It is conditional and requires the willingness and
ability of the other person to give me something that grat-
ifies the sexual side of my nature. *Eros* can never make love
last. Something more is needed.

Phileo

The emotional dimension of love was expressed by the
Greek word *phileo*. *Phileo* referred to the feeling component
of love. When we find ourselves emotionally attracted to
someone because of some attractive quality in that person,
we are experiencing *phileo*. "Falling in love" is most often a
mix of *eros* and *phileo*.

Anyone who has had the experience of "falling in love"
knows how wonderful it is. It is wonderful when this feeling of love toward another person is reciprocated. Almost
every song, movie, and television program glorifies the *phileo*
experience. Much of our cultural concept of love is rooted
in this feeling.

However, the *phileo* dimension of love also has serious
limitations. *Phileo* is an inadequate basis on which to build
a lasting relationship. Emotions are both wonderful and
terrible. Our emotional capability is a God-given gift.
When emotions are operating according to God's plan,
they can be great. But this side of Eden, our emotions tend
to have a life of their own. Emotions are incredibly un-
predictable.

I wake up one morning with wonderfully warm and loving feelings toward my wife; the very next morning I wake
up with no such feelings at all. I might even wake up with
powerfully negative feelings toward my wife. If I am living
my life in a way that allows my feelings to dictate my behavior, I am certain to run into problems.

Most relationships (particularly marriages) go through
a series of stages. Romantic relationships begin with a pe-

riod of enchantment often called "the honeymoon stage."
This is the stage where both *eros* and *phileo* are in full operation. Two people have "fallen in love." They can't seem
to live without each other. They find no flaw in one another. They are floating along on cloud nine. Unfortunately, this stage usually doesn't last very long.

The end of the honeymoon stage begins the morning
after the wedding when, for the first time, the couple sees
each other first thing in the morning. Both discover that
their beloved's "natural beauty" is actually a product of
"better living through chemistry." Puppy love encounters
doggy breath. Reality sets in.

The hard realities of living together move a relationship
into the second stage. This is the stage of disenchantment.
Different relationships will take different lengths of time
to arrive at this stage, and the arrival will be characterized
by different levels of intensity. Entering the disenchantment stage will often lead to a crisis.

Suddenly, at the feeling level, Mr. Right has become Mr.
Wrong. The focus shifts from the half-full glass to the half-
empty glass. Each partner in the marriage discovers a series of irritating habits and behaviors about the other. Sexual attraction begins to fade. At this point the relationship
is about to reach a major crossroad. A decision will be made
whether to abandon the relationship or take whatever actions are necessary to move the relationship into the third
stage—the stage of maturity. The answer to the question
"How do you make love last?" is to be found in the third
dimension of real love.

Stages of Marriage

The honeymoon stage   Disenchantment   Maturity

In recent years the whole arena of romantic love has been attracting the attention of the scientific community. Biochemists have now discovered that the feelings and drives that are associated with romance have definite chemical components. Amazingly, scientists have been able to isolate the chemical produced by the body that stimulates the brain with feelings of passion and romance. The chemical is called phenylethylalanol, or PEA for short.

Along with discovering what has been called "the chemistry of love,"[2] these same scientists have discovered some amazing facts about this chemical process. It appears that in most cases the human biochemical system can only sustain the production of PEA for a period of four years. Biochemically speaking, romantic love has its limitations. Working with cultural anthropologists, these scientists surveyed sixty-five different cultures and found that the peak divorce rate occurred in the fourth year of marriage. Romantic feelings fade. Something more is needed to sustain a relationship and make love last.

Agape

The good news is that something more is possible. The third dimension of love is identified by the Greek word *agape*. This is the Greek word used most frequently in the New Testament to describe the kind of love God expresses toward humanity. *Agape* is quite different from the other two types of love.

The three types of love correspond to the three-dimensional nature of man. *Eros* is a physically based love that originates in the physical dimension of man's nature. *Phileo* is an emotionally based product of the intellectual and feeling dynamics of the soul. *Agape* is spiritually based love that has its source in our relationship with God and the invasion of the human spirit by the Spirit of God.

Three Dimensions and Three Loves

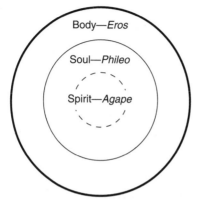

Both *eros* and *phileo* are natural in their origins and expression. *Agape* is supernatural. It is a product of the work of the Holy Spirit in our lives. In the last chapter you were challenged to ask Jesus Christ to come into your life. In the moment that commitment was made you were enabled to love in a new way. With Christ in our lives we are no longer limited to the American myth of sexual and emotional love. To those very good dimensions of love a third and vital dimension has been added: *agape*. *Agape* love is the primary ingredient in a mature and lasting relationship.

Agape love is unconditional. Both *eros* and *phileo* have conditions attached to their expression; they are dependent upon the fulfillment of certain conditions in order for love to continue. *Eros* loves if the loved one gives sexual gratification and remains sexually attractive. *Phileo* loves because of certain lovable traits and characteristics in the loved one; it continues to love as long as those characteristics are present and connecting with the lover's emotional system. But *agape* loves in spite of flaws and inconsistencies. It is unconditionally rooted in the nature of the lover. God's love is like this. It is rooted in his nature, not our lovability. Because Christ now lives in me, I have the ability to love in this same kind of way.

Agape is also volitional. We now have the ability to choose to love even if we are not feeling the emotion we call love. Real love is much more than a feeling. It is a series of actions we choose to take. Real love is a commitment to seek the highest welfare of the person we choose to love. When we choose to love our spouse through periods of disenchantment and crisis we will move into the maturity stage of the marriage. To make love last requires a special kind of love. Only mature love lasts; it must be three-dimensional. *Agape* must be present and dominant.

The Work of Marriage

"Here's a little ditty 'bout Jack and Diane." These words constitute the opening line of John Mellencamp's song "Jack and Diane."[3] John's song is an insightful look at the "all-American" love story. High school sweethearts, living in the heartland of America, are passionately in love. They graduate, marry, and head off on their honeymoon. Then, as Mellencamp observes, "life goes on." Passions fade, reality sets in, life gets tough, and "love" grows cold. The conclusion of the song is often the tragic truth: "Oh yeah, life goes on; long after the thrill of living is gone."

It appears that like millions of teens around our nation and our world, Jack and Diane never learned how to make love last. They entered marriage without anyone explaining the work of love to them.

There are a wide variety of marriages in the world today. There are marriages that end in divorce (almost 50 percent of American marriages end this way). There are marriages where the partners stay together but the relationship is incredibly dysfunctional. There are marriages that exist in a state of peaceful coexistence but where very little love is expressed either physically, emotionally, or spiritually.

Then there are those few marriages where both partners are actually happy and fulfilled in the relationship. These marriages are the ones that are experiencing a nearly mystical quality that the Bible calls "oneness" (see Gen. 2:18–24).

Attaining oneness takes work. When we commit to making our marriages a priority, we commit ourselves to investing the time, energy, and resources necessary for our marriages to become all that God intended them to be. When God designed the marriage relationship, he saw that it was not good for man to be alone. He created woman. He brought the man and woman together and told them that the two were to become one. The formula looks a little crazy: One becomes two in order that the two might become one.

Oneness in marriage is an expression of *agape* love. God created marriage in part to teach people how to love one another. We could think of marriage as a love laboratory. We certainly can learn to love in other contexts. Those who find themselves in the state of singleness don't have to think that if they are not married they will never learn to love. But for those of us who are married, our marriages provide opportunities to learn the most important lesson we can ever learn in life. The work of moving toward oneness in marriage is a labor of love. In the work of learning to become one we will have to learn how to love unconditionally.

I have developed an image of this task of creating oneness that has helped me sort through immature and childish ideas about love and develop a more mature understanding of real love. I picture the husband and wife as two very unique and different gears. Ultimately, these two gears are intended to come together and "mesh" physically, emotionally, and spiritually. The meshing of the gears will then produce something that neither gear has the ability to produce by itself. The simplest and most obvious illustration of this principle is the product of our physical meshing. When we mesh physically we produce children. Most of us are pretty good at this kind of meshing. It is emotional and spiritual meshing that cause us problems.

Around the age of eighteen to twenty, we reach a level of physical maturity. Many of us begin to think about getting married and starting a family. For most, our physical maturity is not matched by emotional and spiritual maturity. Most of us are immature when we marry, and we usually marry someone who is also immature.

Immature people often have immature expectations of marriage. We bring into our marriages certain expectations (usually unconscious) of what a perfect mate should be. For men this ideal mate is some mix of Michelle Pfeiffer, Mother Teresa, and Aunt Jemima. For women the composite may be Mel Gibson, St. Francis of Assisi, and John Paul Getty. The underlying formula is relatively simple: *The ideal mate meets all my needs.*

Having formulated this ideal over the years, we then do a very cruel thing. We project this ideal, with all its expectations, onto our new mate. In most cases my real mate will probably fail to live up to this ideal. My unconscious goal to have all my needs met will get blocked. This will produce a whole series of emotional responses ranging from anger to frustration to depression to discouragement. In other words, I will become disenchanted. This disenchantment manifests itself in an immature person's mind in the form of the thought "Something is wrong with her (or him)."

When this process begins to happen in the life of a man who has committed himself to God's relational priorities, it becomes an opportunity to use *agape* love to move the relationship (and himself) to a new level of maturity. What does the introduction of *agape* into this formula look like?

Agape love is self-sacrificial. It is diametrically opposed to immature love. If I exercise *agape* love, I will no longer think that my wife exists to meet my needs. Marriage becomes a commitment on my part to meet *her* needs. The classic text that defines *agape* love is found in 1 Corinthians, chapter 13. This text says *agape* is not self-seeking (v. 5). Whenever my actions toward my wife reveal self-centeredness, I am not loving with *agape* love. At some point my needs will be in conflict with my wife's needs. When I am letting Jesus Christ live in and through me (which is the secret of releasing *agape* in my life) I will focus on serving my wife's needs rather than my own. Paradoxically, since my greatest needs are for security and significance, loving my mate this way will actually meet my needs in a way an egocentric approach to marriage never could. Once again, it is in losing myself for the sake of Christ and serving instead of seeking to be served, that my own needs are met.

Agape is also accepting. It attempts to know and understand my partner and her needs. *Agape* enables me to accept my wife without constantly attempting to change her. Mature love (or maybe I should say a mature person) has the ability to recognize faulty expectations and perceptions.

I find that the number one false idea in the minds of most men who are struggling with their marriages is that their wife needs to change in order for their marital problems to disappear. This is a tragic lie that not only demeans the wife but also robs the husband of discovering the value of his mate's uniqueness—which is a gift of God to meet his own deepest needs.

Finally, *agape* is self-critical in a positive sense. Instead of focusing on what I think is wrong with my mate, I recognize that the failure of our gears to mesh might be an indication that a few teeth on my own gears need work. Disenchantment, and the conflict or crisis produced by it, leads me to submit myself to God's transforming work in my own life. This process of growth is one of the great benefits of the marriage relationship.

Building a good marriage takes hard work. It takes hard work because marriage is the relationship where the raging monster of self most often raises its ugly head. It is a relationship where the hurt and wounded child of one's past will most frequently make his unexpected and unwanted appearance. It is a relationship where the tendency to ascend the throne of ego and demand to be served most frequently surfaces. Therefore, it is a relationship that provides great possibilities for making hearty strides in our growth toward maturity. For those of us who give our marriages their proper sense of priority, marriage provides a tremendous opportunity to learn to love and serve.

Building a Healthy Marriage

Many excellent books have been written on the subject of marriage. Rather than attempting to exhaustively deal with the subject, I would like to give you a few hints of how Allison and I have tried to make our marriage a priority.

Commitment

In the fall of 1982 Allison and I entered a period of major disenchantment in our marriage that led to a crisis. Small unresolved issues in our relationship had been building for years. Allison began to experience severe bouts of depression that she believed were my fault. I was experiencing unbearable frustration with Allison. The building tension between us reached a climax on Thanksgiving Day. What should have been a minor conflict escalated into a major crisis. By the end of the day we both knew that if something didn't change we were headed for divorce.

God often graciously intervenes in our lives when we least expect it and certainly don't deserve it. Such was the case in our lives in 1982. Instead of making a foolish decision, we made a wise (and I believe gracious in the truest sense of the word) choice. We decided that we could not solve our problems by ourselves. We came to the mutual decision to seek professional help. That was one of the most difficult decisions I ever made. It started a process of professional counseling that was equally difficult. The counseling process lasted four years.

During those four years there were many occasions when each of us felt like throwing in the towel. There were many times when we were convinced that our marriage was never going to work. There were days when the most exotic forms of torture known to man seemed preferable to staying married. Through all of those difficult times it was raw commitment that provided the glue that kept our marriage together. Commitment provided the time we needed to work through serious disenchantment and move into a new level of love and maturity in our marriage.

When Allison and I first discussed getting married (in what now seems "long ago in a galaxy far away"), we made the commitment that our vow of "till death do us part" would be taken seriously. We both came from families in which divorce had left us in single-parent homes. We decided that divorce would not be an option for us.

This decision was rooted in our relationship with Christ. Even in the most difficult times of conflict we both desired to live in obedience to the clear teaching of Jesus in this area. I have no doubt that our mutual, spiritually based commitment was the primary human factor that saved our marriage. Without this kind of commitment, the temptation to push the "eject button" during the crisis times of the disenchantment stage would have been too great to resist.

We not only committed to staying in the relationship, we committed to making the relationship as much like God's design as possible. It is hard enough to simply stay together, but staying together was not our only goal. We wanted to have a good marriage. That commitment required time, energy, and resources. Part of our payoff came on January 5, 1994, when we celebrated our twentieth anniversary. It never would have happened without commitment.

Communication

In order for our marriage to grow and thrive, we needed help learning to communicate more effectively. If commitment is the foundation of a lasting relationship, then communication provides the framework. Marriage was designed to be a life-sharing experience. Communication is how we share our lives.

The most helpful tool we have developed in this area of communication is our date night. We set aside one evening a week to go out together. We try to keep this date religiously. Communication doesn't occur without time spent together. We leave our wonderful children at home and spend the evening together. Since Allison and I both enjoy movies, our date often involves going to a movie and out to dinner. To avoid a midlife crisis at age forty, I bought a Harley-Davidson motorcycle at age thirty-nine. At first Allison chose not to get on the back of this particular piece of machinery while it propelled my body down the road at breakneck speed. Then one day she broke down and agreed to go for a ride with me. She got hooked! Now, there is nothing we would rather do than climb on the Harley and head off for a ride together. We spend hours at a time with large grins on our faces. These are the times we make sure we are in touch with what is going on in each other's lives and in our marriage. They also are times of simply having fun and enjoying one another.

At other times during the week we might need to lock ourselves in our bedroom and hash out issues that are creating problems. It always amazes me how I have a tendency to let little issues build until I lose perspective. I tend to let things slide because I hate conflict. Ali is great about initiating conflict resolution. Talking through areas and issues of conflict has a way of diffusing them. Communication is a critical component in the building of a healthy marriage.

For many men the communication component does not come easily. A wife often wants to share her deepest feelings; most men, myself included, have been programmed to be relatively out of touch with their feelings. The ability to communicate at a feeling level often has to be learned with the help of a professional. Periodically, when Ali and I are at a stalemate in our communication process, we go back for several weeks of professional counseling to help us move to deeper maturity and intimacy. This is always a difficult and humbling experience for me, but the product is so beneficial that I highly recommend paying the price.

Caring

In a world that couldn't care less, marriage was designed to be a relationship where two people couldn't care more. Perhaps no other ingredient, except a lot of grace, is more essential in building a healthy marriage than a commitment to care.

I am a great fan of Mother Teresa. Every time I read an article about her or see an account of what she is doing, I find myself tremendously challenged. Several years ago I was reading a short biography of her life and work.[4] I was so over-whelmed by the beauty of her life of service that I made a decision. I decided that the real action was in Calcutta. I decided that to really live the Christian life I needed to go to India to serve the poorest of the poor with Mother Teresa.

I happened to be standing in the kitchen at the time I had this great idea. I had what I believe was an encounter with God. Although his voice was not audible, I had as strong an impression in my mind as if an audible voice had spoken. I "heard" God say, "Look around you. You don't need to go to Calcutta. You can do what Mother Teresa does right in your home."

At the time our daughter Stephanie was still in diapers. Moms with small kids have one of the toughest jobs in the world! On this particular day Allison had not had time to even think about doing the dishes. I was ready to head to Calcutta to love lepers, but I had neglected to care enough to clean the kitchen.

Mother Teresa often explains her work on the basis of Jesus' teaching that whatever we do for one of the least of our brothers we do for Christ (Matt. 25:40). When she sees a dying person, a leper on the street, or an unwanted child, she thinks, "There is Jesus in a distressing disguise." The day after my "revelation," I happened to be upstairs in my daughter's room when she had a monumental experience of filling her diaper. I looked at her and thought, "There is Jesus in a distressing disguise." It is hard to explain, but somehow I had a bit more joy in changing that diaper.

Marriage is a relationship that thrives on caring. I confess that I have light-years to go in this area myself. I am much more eager to be served than to serve. But I have observed over the last few years that the quality of my relationship with Allison is usually a direct reflection of how I am working out the caring commitment. When I care, I am loving with *agape* love. When I serve, I am expressing the spirit of Christ. The purpose of life is to love and to serve. Marriage is a love laboratory where God wants to teach us and bless us if we will give our marriages their proper place of priority within God's divine blueprint.

Personal Reflection

If we are married, there is no area of our lives that provides more fertile soil for assessment and adjustment than our relationships with our mates. Here are a few suggestions for putting the ideas contained in this chapter into practice:

1. Find a copy of your marriage vows and read them carefully.
2. Evaluate the strength of each type of love in your marriage.
3. Read 1 Corinthians 13 every day for a month.
4. Pray about what "gears" in your life God might want to change.
5. Schedule a date night with your spouse this week.
6. If your marriage is in trouble, get help!

Buy a Harley!

And Other Tips on Fathering

Wednesday morning, April 9, 1986, an article appeared in the *Rocky Mountain News* entitled "Rewards of Fatherhood Often Discovered Too Late." The author of the article related the story of how he responded to a friend's complaint about his wife "nagging" him to spend more time with their kids. The writer shared how he wanted to "punch his buddy right between the eyes" but didn't. He observed that some lessons could only be learned the hard way.

The columnist went on to reflect on his own failure as a father. He had found it hard to take time to give his kids a bath or wrestle on the floor with them. He shared, with painful honesty, about his reluctance to break away from watching a ball game to read them a bedtime story. Before he knew it his children were grown and able to bathe themselves. They stopped wanting to wrestle on the floor.

110

The time came when they were much too grown up to have Dad read them a bedtime story. That's when the fact hit him, "right between the eyes," that the rewards of fatherhood are often discovered too late!

That article held special significance for me. At five-thirty that Wednesday morning, just about the time the newspaper containing that article was landing in the driveway of our home, a brand-new, bouncing baby boy by the name of Baker Theodore Beltz was born. I felt like the timing of the article was a message from God. I clipped the article and put it in my file labeled "Dads" to serve as a constant reminder that my children are a gift of God, intended to be a vital priority in my relational network.

I suppose many people have had memorable New Year's Eves. There is one I will never forget. At about eleven-thirty on the morning of December 31, 1979, my wife, Allison, began to have contractions. The contractions progressed mildly throughout the day. That evening, as the contractions grew closer together and more intense, we packed our little car and headed toward Rose Hospital. While the rest of the world was watching the crowds gathered in Times Square, we were heavy into Lamaze breathing techniques. Shortly after the clock struck twelve, we headed toward the delivery room. Early in the morning of the first day of a new decade our daughter, Stephanie, was born. I still vividly remember holding my precious little girl in my arms, wondering what she needed from me and what it meant to be a dad.

It seems like only yesterday, and yet as I write these words, that little "baby" is a freshman in high school! Over the years the challenges and rewards of fatherhood have been a major part of living out the divine design in my own life. The birth of Baker more than doubled the challenges and exponentially increased the rewards. Through these years I have learned some of the answers to those critical questions I wondered about on that New Year's Day so long ago.

The Primary Task of Fathering

I remember walking out of the hospital that cold and snowy New Year's Day and heading for my car to drive home. As I began to cross the street the strangest thought entered my mind. Without warning, the words "life insurance" popped onto the screen of my consciousness. I don't believe I had ever given life insurance a thought before that moment. But now I was a dad. What do dads do? They are providers and protectors; ergo, life insurance.

Although providing and protecting are two of my responsibilities as a father, neither of those responsibilities is my primary task in the divine blueprint. My primary task as a dad who takes his marching orders from Jesus Christ is to bless my children. I am to be the human vehicle through whom God touches the lives of my children with a powerful spiritual reality that produces spiritual empowerment and emotional wholeness in their lives.

In the patriarchal society of ancient Israel, this experience of blessing was to be transmitted from father to son, generation to generation. Genesis 12 relates how God entered into a redemptive covenant with a man named Abraham. That covenant ultimately found fulfillment in the person and work of Jesus Christ and the gift of regeneration and transformation made possible by the indwelling presence of the Holy Spirit. God said to Abraham:

I will bless you. . . .
You will be a (source of) blessing . . .
Through you all nations (humanity) will be blessed.

Genesis 12:1–3 (author's own translation)

This covenant was worked out by a process that was intimately related to the father-child relationship. The intended scenario was:

God blesses Abraham > Abraham becomes a blessed father > Abraham blesses his son > His son grows to become a blessed father > He blesses his son > His son grows to become a blessed father > etc.

Obviously, something went wrong somewhere. But God's design from the beginning was that the primary job of a dad was to bless his children. What does this look like?

In their book, *The Blessing*, Gary Smalley and John Trent attempt to take this ancient concept and translate it for contemporary application.[1] They break down the impartation of blessing into five components. For the sake of our discussion, I will synthesize the five into three: time, tenderness, and truth. They are the dynamics which must be present in our relationships with our children if we are to meet their deepest needs and fulfill our primary task as fathers.

The Gift of Time

When we come to grips with the fact that life is short, we begin to realize that one of our most valuable possessions is time. Every choice I make about how I spend my day involves the use of this limited resource. Over the years I have come to understand how my children desperately need a healthy chunk of that time.

In the Old Testament Book of Deuteronomy, Moses delivered a series of messages to the people of Israel as they finally prepared to enter and possess the promised land. With Israel camped on the east bank of the Jordan River, Moses issued a command that became a creedal statement for the nation. Moses said, "Hear, O Israel: The LORD our God, the LORD is one. Love the LORD your God with all your heart and with all your soul and with all your strength" (Deut. 6:4–5). This was the Scripture text Jesus quoted when asked about the greatest commandment.

Although I was familiar with this command, I was surprised to see what immediately follows the command. Moses challenged the people of Israel to impress these commandments on their own hearts and then to impress them on their children. He told the parents to accomplish this task by talking about them to their children when they sat at home, when they walked along the road, when they went to bed, and when they woke up. The impartation of God's truth was not to occur in a classroom setting, but in the context of parents and their children spending quality time together. The destiny of the nation of Israel depended on it. Families were to become what Edith Schaeffer calls a "relay of truth."[2]

There is a significant difference, of course, between the culture of that day and our own. In those days moms and dads and boys and girls spent a lot of time together. Living in a primarily rural and agricultural society, children often worked alongside their fathers in the field or alongside their mothers in the home. Many of the distractions of our modern society didn't even exist in ancient Israel. What was the *norm* in ancient times must be *cultivated* in our culture.

This challenge was illustrated for me in an article published in *Scientific American* magazine. Entitled "The Origins of Alienation," the article reported the results of a study involving families with preschool children.[3] The intention of the study was to discover how much time fathers of preschool children were spending in quality interaction with their children. The fathers were first asked to estimate how much time they were spending on a daily basis with their children. The average reported response was an estimated fifteen to twenty minutes a day. This, in and of itself, seems like a tragic answer. The real tragedy emerged as those conducting the study actually monitored the interaction of these fathers with their children. The results of the study were staggering. The actual amount of time these children were being given by their fathers amounted to 2.7 encounters daily, consisting of an average cumulative elapsed time of thirty-seven seconds! Thirty-seven seconds a day during the period of development where personality, psychosexual development, and identity are at their most formative stages. Recent studies show that the average preschooler in America spends twenty-five to thirty hours a week in front of a television set. No wonder our kids are confused and in trouble!

Sometimes when I remember the above passage in Deuteronomy, I think about days when I have to be at an early morning meeting and then work straight through into the late evening. On those days I don't see my children awake. I have lost an entire day of influence in my children's lives and am robbed of the joy of simply enjoying them. I hate those days and I am glad that they are few and far between. Unfortunately, for some dads and their kids, days like those are the rule rather than the exception.

I also think about those days when I come home from work and just want to get in a fetal position and be left alone. At those times I remember a line from a documentary called *The Family Gone Wild*. The film includes a scene in which Dr. Gary Demarest comes home after a long day at work feeling the way I just described. His sixth grade daughter is waiting for him in the driveway, hoping to play tetherball with her dad. Every fiber of his being wants to hit the couch and "veg out." Dr. Demarest makes the observation that the principle in his life that gives him the motivation to go out and play tetherball is "When I get home, I begin the most important work of the day."[4]

I am one of those lucky guys who actually enjoys his job. My work is filled with significant activity. I teach, counsel, write, speak at retreats and workshops, and help provide leadership for a growing and dynamic church. All of those tasks are important. I also am very aware that God has the ability to raise up others who are able to perform those tasks better than I. But I am the only daddy that Baker and Stephanie have. If I fail at my job as a father, no one else can, or will, fill that void. This is the most important work of my day, to love my wife and children and to be involved in a significant way in their lives. That will only take place when there is a significant investment of time in these relationships. It takes time together with our children to bless them.

Smalley and Trent say that meaningful touch and spoken words are two of the components necessary to give our children the blessing.[5] I was reminded of these recently as I spent a great day with my son.

For the second year in a row, I headed out of Denver with my son to go to the National Men's Conference in Boulder. It was a beautiful Saturday morning in Colorado, and Baker and I decided to ride to the conference on my Harley. As Baker held on for dear life, the words "meaningful touch" took on a whole new spin. We rode and talked and went to the conference. After the morning session, we rode into the mountains to have lunch at a small cafe. On the way back we stopped and walked along a railroad track, waiting to watch trains while Baker hunted for hidden treasure. It was an entire morning of talk and touch and time together. I was blessing my son.

The Gift of Tenderness

There is nothing magical about time spent with our children, in and of itself. What is important is what goes on during that time. Sitting in the same room with our children while we all watch television might be enjoyable, but it is rarely what you could call quality time.

One of the classic biblical texts on parenting is found in the New Testament Book of Ephesians. In the sixth chapter of this little book the apostle Paul instructs us to raise our children "in the training and instruction of the Lord" (Eph. 6:4 NIV). The word in the Greek text that is translated "raise them up" or "bring them up" is the word *ektrepho*. This word means "to nurture or to nourish." It implies an attitude of care, provision, and support. Nurture is the care and tenderness given to a person for the purpose of facilitating his or her health and growth.

Dr. Ross Campbell, in his excellent book *How to Really Love Your Child*, gives several suggestions about how to build nurturing relationships.[6] Dr. Campbell says that in order to have quality time with our children, we must work at giving focused attention. The most basic characteristic of focused attention is eye contact. It always amazes me to note the difference between just being around my children and having this kind of eyeball-to-eyeball interaction with them. Stephanie taught me this lesson early in my fathering education.

I am a reasonably good early-morning person. When Stephanie was a toddler, she used to get up two or three times in the middle of the night and then arise for the day at about five-thirty in the morning. In order to survive this schedule, Allison and I struck a deal. Ali took the "night shift" and I took on early-morning duty so that Ali could catch up on her sleep after these frequent middle-of-the-night episodes with Stephanie.

I actually looked forward to these early-morning times with my daughter. I also began to develop a little routine that ended up teaching me a lesson about focused attention. The two essential items in my early-morning routine in those days were a cup of hot coffee and the morning paper. I would turn on a children's program on T.V. (educational, of course) and settle onto the couch with paper and coffee to "spend a little time with Stephanie." I even developed the skill of responding to Stephanie's many questions without losing my place in the paper.

One morning as I was going through my "yes, Sweety" response to one of those profound two-year-old inquiries about the nature of life and the universe, I had a startling experience. Stephanie had figured out my game. She ripped the paper out of my hand so that I was staring eyeball-to-eyeball with my beautiful little girl. The message was clear! She wanted my focused attention, not just my physical presence.

Stephanie sleeps in these days. My new morning buddy is Baker. I am usually up and well into my new morning routine when he gets up. But when I hear him coming down the stairs toward the living room, I put down whatever I am doing and gear up for some focused attention.

Giving focused attention is a commitment to nurturing. I find that it requires a conscious decision to enter into the world of my children. It usually means doing things that I wouldn't think of doing otherwise. For Baker that means riding bikes, building projects, and playing ball together. For Stephanie that used to mean being willing to play Barbie dolls with her. That probably isn't too macho, but that is what it means to be a daddy.

I recently ran across a survey called "A Good Father." A group of children had been asked to finish the sentence, "A good father. . . ." The survey revealed the following list of answers:

A good father . . .
helps kids learn to ride a bike
reads stories to the kids
says "don't eat mud"
loves

explains when asked to explain
goes to church and Sunday school
is home a lot
listens
protects me
lets my friends come in to play
takes me fishing
disciplines me
helps me
spends time with me
holds me
doesn't go away

It seems kind of crazy that the things that really matter to children are so simple. They long for nurturing time from their parents, time that includes eye contact and tender touch, time when we leave the adult world and enter the world of children, time sitting on the floor playing with trucks and dolls.

Nurturing also involves the messages we send our children both verbally and nonverbally. Stephanie is no longer a little girl; she is now a young woman. To be more precise, she is a teenager. Over the years, Allison and I have attempted to affirm her by sending messages that express to her how much we value her.

Recently I became aware that I wasn't doing as good a job at this with Stephanie as I used to. It seems that there is much more raw material for criticism in the lives of our teenage children than there is for affirmation. I began to consciously reestablish patterns of affirmation and, in the process, stumbled into a great technique.

I do much of my studying and writing in my office at home. This office happens to be located next to Stephanie's bedroom. Stephanie loves to come into the office when

I'm not around to tinker with my computer and, of course, use my phone! I have a program on the computer called After Dark. This program is a screen saver that automatically puts the computer to sleep and puts moving objects on the screen. I have flying toasters, colorful fish, and shooting stars and a whole host of options on this program. One of the options allows you to put messages on the screen that repeatedly float across the monitor in a variety of colors. Stephanie and I began to use this program as a high-tech vehicle of communication.

I would put a message on the screen like "Stephanie: a young woman of sterling character and graceful bearing." I would return home to find the following on the screen: "Yuk! Gag me with a spoon!"

One day I decided to get both theological and etymological, so I put the following message on the screen: "Stephanie; from the Greek *stephanos*, meaning crowned one; i.e., queen or princess." I was convinced that Stephanie would be blessed by such a thoughtful and scholarly electronic affirmation. When I came home that evening I found Stephanie's response: "Old men like you lose their hair and buy big toys to make up for it!"

I didn't say this would be easy! But if we can keep working at being nurturing, we give our children two priceless gifts. The first is the gift of a positive, biblical sense of self-esteem. There can be little doubt that the quality of our children's lives will be directly related to self-esteem. This gift is a direct product of the quality of nurturing time we give them.

Many of us lacked this kind of nurture growing up. We have paid the price for this deficiency both emotionally and relationally. We were not blessed. Growing up in non-nurturing families we developed either low self-esteem or no self-esteem. Much of our unconscious motivations in adult life are attempts to prove that we are really valuable. We must remember that we are the products of products.

As the Bible reminds us, the sins of the fathers have been visited on the children. But we have a chance to break the cycle. If as parents we can simply make a difference in this area of nurturing and build self-esteem into our children, then they will experience a quality of life much more positive than we experienced. And we hope (and pray) that they will continue this process in the nurturing of their children. We can thereby set in motion a positive pattern of quality nurturing that will bear fruit for generations to come.

The Gift of Truth

The greatest gift we give our children is a vital and healthy relationship with God. The most important hour in our house used to begin around eight o'clock each evening. At that time we began the process (or should I say battle?) of getting our children into bed. It was also the time when we tried to have a period of focused spiritual input in their lives.

As the father in our home I believe God has given me a unique role in bringing spiritual blessing to my children. I long to lead them into a vital and positive relationship with God. I know that at some point there will be personal decisions they will have to make on their own. I also know that what happens in our home in these early years will lay a foundation on which those later decisions will be based.

When Stephanie was born I began a very simple ritual every night. The final encounter of my day with her was to hold her in my arms and pray for her. I would always end my prayer by praying over her the Levitical blessing found in the Old Testament Book of Numbers:

The LORD bless you and keep you;
the LORD make his face shine upon you

and be gracious to you;
the LORD turn his face toward you
and give you peace.

Numbers 6:24–26

God gave this prayer to the priesthood of Israel to bless the nation. As the "priest" of my family, I have used it to ask the Lord to bless my children.

In addition to praying for Stephanie, Allison and I would rock her and sing spiritual songs of praise and worship. We wanted to fill her little mind and spirit with positive input as she drifted off to sleep each night. As she grew older we read to her the normal stories of childhood, including stories about God's love for her. Above all else I wanted to impart to her a positive image of God as the one who above all others loves her and cares for her. As the years have rolled by it has been an ongoing challenge to find age-appropriate and interesting ways to keep this process going.

When Baker came along the challenge doubled. Each of our children is so unique that we need to find the vehicle of truth that is most effective with him or her. Baker still loves to listen to Bible stories. He won't go to sleep at night until both Mom and Dad have prayed for him. I am always astonished at the amount of spiritual perception he has at his young age.

When I think back on those questions I asked the day Stephanie was born, I realize that what our children need from us is the gift of truth. The family is a "relay of truth." The impartation and modeling of life-changing and life-shaping truth is the job of the family.

When I was in high school I ran on our school track team. I was a member of several relay teams. The critical seconds in a relay race involve the few short feet when one runner passes the baton to the next runner. Our team often won races against much faster teams because we won the race on the precision of the baton transfer. Other times we lost races against teams with slower runners by fumbling the baton in the handoff.

Life is like a relay race. God has handed us the baton of truth. He has entrusted us with the lives of our children and instructed us to pass the baton. Part of that exchange will involve verbal instruction. Part of that exchange will involve the process of discipline. Most of the exchange will be a matter of prayer and example. Our children will learn what they live. Giving our children the gift of truth will require the ongoing discipline of working the truth out in our own lives.

Every once in a while we have an experience that lets us know how the "race" is going. One morning I was having my morning time of prayer and Bible study in my favorite chair in the living room. (By now you might have guessed that I am a bit off center; let me confirm your hunch. My favorite chair is an old overstuffed easy chair that my wife and I found at a secondhand store. We had it recovered in black and white cowhide. It used to sit in our living room next to a 1952 Seeburg jukebox. We had an old Coke machine in one corner of the living room, and I kept my Harley-Davidson motorcycle in the other corner. This environment was highlighted by one wall of the living room that was all glass and looked out on a perfect view of the front range of the Rocky Mountains. This was the spot where I did my best praying, thinking, and writing.)

On this particular morning I had finished praying and was working on a chapter of a previous book. Baker came running into the living room as soon as he awoke. We were in a stretch where the first thing he wanted to do in the morning was climb up in my lap and sit for a while. I took full advantage of this special period of grace!

Seeing me writing, Baker stopped and asked why I was working. I replied that I had not finished the work I needed to do the day before. He asked, "Are you not finished because I sat too long on your lap?" I saw an opportunity to use his question to affirm my love for him and his value to me, so I answered, "Nothing in the whole world is more important than you sitting on my lap." I saw a grin spread across his face as he said, "That's wrong, Dad." I was stunned, so I asked, "What do you mean?" Baker replied, "God is more important, Dad!" Pretty good theology for a five-year-old!

I had an idea of how I could use this reply to teach him another lesson, so I said, "Baker, do you know how Daddy likes to sit in this chair each morning and read his Bible and pray?" Baker shook his head in the affirmative. "Well, that's kind of like Dad sitting in God's lap," I said. Baker smiled broadly and exclaimed, "Cool, Dad!" That little encounter was a huge affirmation that the gift of truth was taking root in his life.

Like it or not, many of our children's unconscious ideas and feelings about a heavenly Father will be shaped and influenced by their experience of their earthly father. I'm sure that at the age of five, Baker envisioned God as some kind of giant, blown-up version of me. Therefore, my own relationship with Christ needs to be vital and positive if I am effectively to give Baker and Stephanie the gift of truth.

Time, tenderness, and truth: three gifts that our children desperately need. Gifts that, when given with consistency, produce in the lives of our children the spiritual reality the Bible calls "the blessing." These three gifts have the potential of facilitating in our children's lives the two most significant qualities we can impart as parents: a positive and healthy view of God, and a healthy, biblical sense of self-esteem. If we are successful in passing along these gifts, we will have helped our children begin at an early age to live according to the divine blueprint and avoid many of the pitfalls that come with getting hooked into the Solomon Syndrome.

Personal Reflection

Here are a few questions to think about and ideas to try in your effort to build this rung on your ladder of love:

1. Monitor your time with your kids this week; how much time are you investing in your children on a daily basis?
2. Are you giving your children focused attention? Work on practicing eye contact and gentle touch with your kids.
3. Pray with your children before they go to bed this week. Touch their heads gently and ask God to bless them.
4. Plan a fun outing this weekend.
5. Go to church as a family.

9

Hanging Out at Grace's Place

Reflections on the Subject of Buddies

There was an old yellow Porsche parked in my girl-friend's driveway. Actually, the driveway technically belonged to a *former* girlfriend that I still had an immense crush on. The year was 1970 and I was home from college on spring break. The presence of the Porsche confirmed the rumors.

For several years I had been wrestling with the issue of what life was all about. Like many of my contemporaries I was looking for answers in some very strange places. I had listened to the voices that criticized the shallow materialism of the establishment and that advocated drugs, sex, and rock and roll as the pathway to freedom and meaning. My former girlfriend, Sydna, had enough intelligence to analyze the changes taking place in my life and tell me to get lost.

Then I began to hear the stories. Some of my old school friends had become "Jesus freaks." I probably wouldn't have paid much attention to the rumors except that my old flame was part of the group. Not only had she become a Christian (I had no idea what this even meant), she was actually dating the youth minister who was leading this new religious movement so many of my old schoolmates were caught up in. His name was Richard Beach. The Porsche was his, and so was my old girlfriend.

I first met Rich on the Fourth of July, 1970. I was with a group of friends who had gone to a party at an abandoned rock quarry outside Kansas City. It was a notorious hang-out for the "turn on, tune in, and drop out" crowd. Upon arriving at the quarry I was delighted to see a rock band, complete with generators, ready to crank up the tunes. It looked like it was going to be a great afternoon. Then I saw them: the Jesus freaks. It was a setup! The band was with them and so was Sydna.

Everyone gathered around to hear the band play. When the band finished, Rich stood and addressed the crowd. He talked about Jesus Christ. He also told the crowd that a couple of the people with him wanted to tell us what Christ meant in their lives. I distinctly remember two of the people who shared their stories that afternoon. One was a fellow by the name of Bud Abel. Bud had recently retired from his career as outside linebacker for the Kansas City Chiefs. His presence and story quickly silenced any would-be hecklers in the crowd. Even though I was feeling a little rowdy myself, I decided to be on my best behavior.

After Bud finished, Rich introduced Sydna. She stood in front of this crowd and told how Jesus Christ had changed her life. I can't remember much of what she said, but I remember thinking she looked about as cute as it was possible for a girl to look. It really bugged me that she was dating this guy Rich instead of me.

When Sydna finished speaking Rich rose again and explained how it was possible to have a personal relationship with Jesus Christ. He invited anyone who wanted to talk further to stick around for a while. I saw my opportunity. I wasn't buying into this Jesus stuff for a minute, but I thought that with my arsenal of arguments, finely honed from a semester of college philosophy, this might be my chance to win back Sydna's affection.

For the next forty-five minutes it was the Christians against the lions! I certainly wish someone would have taped that discussion. I tried to baffle Rich with lofty philosophical arguments; he responded with brief but kind responses, always punctuated with a verse from the Bible. I wasn't always able to figure out how his response fit my argument. Later, I decided that he was attempting to plant spiritual seeds in my life hoping that they might bear fruit at some later time.

When our discussion was finished, we shook hands. Rich told me that God loved me and that he did, too. I thought at the time that this was a pretty strange thing for one guy to say to another guy. All I could manage to say in response was a shallow and meaningless "I love you, too."

I didn't convince Rich to give up his Christian faith, and I didn't convince Sydna to give up Rich. I actually left the rock quarry feeling like I had done a pretty good job of making Rich's faith look foolish. I had no idea that by the time the Fourth of July rolled around again, Rich Beach would become the best friend I had ever had.

Over the next few months my life went great. I moved into a slick apartment with one of my good friends. I was doing well in my work at the university. I was dating some of the cutest girls in school. I had a nice new Volkswagen bug with a great stereo. I couldn't have written a better script for my life. There was only one problem; it wasn't working. I still felt an emptiness and restlessness inside. My life lacked an adequate sense of meaning, purpose, and direction. Something was missing.

By the fall of 1970 I decided that I had to figure this out once and for all. I decided that every weekend I would visit a different church, synagogue, mosque, or temple until I knew whether or not there was a valid spiritual dimension to life. My first visit proved "fatal." I visited the church where Rich, Sydna, Bud, and the other folks from the rock quarry went. The pastor was a great guy by the name of Ted Nissen. I had actually met Ted before when he was visiting our campus to see some of the students who attended Colonial Presbyterian Church. I thought that going to hear Ted speak was a logical place to begin my pilgrimage. I also thought it might give me a chance to sneak another peek at Sydna.

My plan was to sit in the back of church and cruise out the door as soon as the service was over. I didn't want any of the gang from the rock quarry to know I was there. The plan was foiled by one of my former wrestling buddies from high school. Bob spotted me and sat next to me in the service. He also invited me to come out and play football with the church team the following Saturday. I told him I would try, even though eight o'clock on a Saturday morning seemed a bit difficult to make, given the events I had planned for Friday night.

Nonetheless, the following Saturday I showed up to play football with the Colonial team against another church team. During the game, a fight broke out between the two church groups. I found myself looking at all these guys rolling around on the ground wrestling with each other. I remember saying to myself, "I think I could be a Christian!"

That morning was the beginning of a relationship with a group of young men that eventually led me to start attending a Bible study for college students. At the study I continued to hear about the difference between man's attempts at being religious (which was my concept of what it meant to be a Christian) and a real relationship with Jesus Christ.

By the second week of November I had thought a great deal about what it would mean to commit my life to Jesus Christ. I had started to count the cost. I knew that much of my lifestyle was inconsistent with what Christ would want for my life. I knew that I would have to make, or allow Christ to make, big changes in my ethical and moral conduct. I knew I would have to give up "altering my state of consciousness" and change much of my dating behavior. I thought I could handle most of that. My biggest worry was the fear that I would probably lose all my buddies.

At first some of my friends shared my interest in investigating spiritual things. That was still "hip" in the early seventies. As I became more serious about the claims of Christ and what they might mean for my life, my friends decided to get back to the party life. I was pretty sure that a decision to receive Christ as Savior and follow him as Lord would mean losing the friendships I had developed over the years. I had no idea at the time that Christ would be able to fill the void created by this loss with a quality of friendship I had never before experienced.

The fateful night arrived in that second week of November. I was sitting in my room reading the Gospel of John. Suddenly, unexpectedly, truth hit me in a way it never had before. I had one of those rare moments of mental and spiritual clarity and I knew that Jesus was who he claimed to be. I knew he lived and died for me and rose again. I knew he was alive and had the power to invade my life. I even knew that he had a plan for my life if I was willing to surrender myself to him. I vividly remember thinking, "If all this is true, nothing in all the world is more important than making this decision." I dropped to my knees at the side of the bed and began to pray. I said something like, "Lord, I have tried to run my life for twenty-one years and I'm not doing a very good job of it.

I really need you. Thank you for dying on the cross for me. Please come into my life, Lord Jesus." It really was that simple. He came. I know; I was there!

I don't believe it always happens this way, but for me, receiving Christ did mean the loss of many old friends. But God filled that void with the gift of true friendship. A small group of Christian men began to teach me what it's like to have real friends.

Cheers!

When I think about the role friendship has played in my life since that night in 1970, I am reminded of the T.V. show *Cheers*. One night, during the first season of the show, I happened to be walking through the family room when the theme song for the show came on the air. The words really hit home. They described a place where "everybody knows your name," a place where people share common struggles and are genuinely glad you are there.

I remember thinking how tragic it was to waste such a great song on a T.V. show about a bar. I thought that song should be the anthem of the church. Unfortunately, in the imperfect world in which we live, some bars may provide better fellowship than some of our churches. That is not the way it was intended to be. Fortunately, that was not my experience.

Over the last twenty-plus years I have had the great blessing of friends who have radically improved the quality of my life. They have taught me the true meaning of friendship. They have also helped me realize how critical the friendship rung on the ladder of love is in experiencing the quality of life that God intended for us. My Christian friends have challenged, encouraged, instructed, and shared the journey of living a life that counts. They have taken me to what I call "Grace's Place." Grace's Place is a spiritual reality in which the theme song from *Cheers* finds fulfillment. It is a network of relationships that is always there when "making your way in the world today" has taken everything you've got. It is a place where a small group of men "know your name" and are "always glad you came." Grace's Place is a metaphor for the priority of friendship within the relational network God has designed to meet our real needs.

Seven Qualities of Authentic Friendship

The quality of relationship it takes to have a Grace's Place experience in your life is what the New Testament calls fellowship. Fellowship is our English translation of the Greek word *koinonia*. *Koinonia* means "sharing in common." Authentic fellowship is a sharing of our lives with other people.

Several years ago Louis Evans Jr., then pastor of National Presbyterian Church in Washington, D.C., wrote a book called *Creative Love*.[1] In the book, Dr. Evans articulated the principles his church attempted to follow in what he calls covenant groups. A covenant group is an organizational attempt to create authentic friendship and fellowship. The covenants to which these groups commit themselves bear a striking resemblance to the commitments John Wesley built into his class meetings during the time of the Great Awakening. If we can develop a few friendships characterized by these qualities we will be a long way toward discovering our own Grace's Place.

Quality One: Unconditional Love

If my relationship with Rich Beach has taught me anything about authentic friendship, it is that an authentic friendship must be built on the foundation of unconditional love. Before meeting Rich I had never experienced an unconditional friendship. What often pass for friendships in our culture are actually relationships of convenience and mutual usefulness. We develop these "friendships" based on what someone can do for us or how the relationship will help us get ahead in the rat race. Most of these relationships are highly conditional.

I know about these kind of relationships. In my "misspent youth" I wanted to be friends with people who would help me look good (a difficult task at the time). I wanted to run around with the "in group" and the "cool" kids so that I would be identified with them. If someone didn't measure up to my criteria in these areas, I didn't have time or energy for them.

This approach to relationships is incredibly destructive. Not only is it destructive for the person who doesn't quite measure up to our standard, it is destructive to our own inner life. It is a vivid exercise in human self-centeredness. Every time we act along these lines we reinforce negative dynamics in our inner lives. What often passes for friendship in such a scenario is simply two people using each other. My relationship with Rich was not like that.

It didn't take long for me to realize that Rich liked me for me. I had very little to offer him; I could not have improved his image or his social standing. But Rich couldn't have cared less about those kinds of things. His whole approach to our relationship was one of unconditional love. He was committed to my highest welfare and spiritual growth. He became a human vehicle through whom the unconditional love of Christ was expressed.

Rich became more than a friend. He was a spiritual mentor who helped me grow through the difficult early years of my relationship with Christ. Sydna got away (from both of us!), but our friendship has lasted through the years.

Quality Two: Availability

It is a great gift to have a friend like Rich. Many people go through a whole lifetime without ever having one friend of this caliber. I have had the good fortune of knowing several. In the spring of 1980 I met Bo Mitchell. His friendship changed the course of my life.

Bo was a successful young businessman when we met. We teamed up to develop a ministry to nonchurched businessmen and their families. For over ten years Bo and I had the pleasure of speaking at men's retreats around the nation, sharing many of the principles contained in these pages.

In the early days of our friendship Bo used to say, "Everything I have is yours, except my wife." He meant it. If my car broke down, Bo considered it his problem. When I couldn't find a publisher for my first book, *How to Survive the End of the World*, Bo put up the money to self-publish the book. Together we became Full Court Press. When Allison and I were going through our marital struggles, Bo called every day and encouraged me to "hang in there." When the idea for Cherry Hills Community Church seemed to be a calling from God, Bo put every ounce of his energy, creativity, ability, and resources into making the church a reality.

Bo taught me and modeled the covenant of availability for me. Over the years I had the opportunity to reciprocate in small ways. When the economy of Denver went into a tailspin, Bo lost virtually everything. On several occasions Allison and I made our resources available to help Bo make it through tough times. Friendship begins to get very gutsy at these levels.

When my son was in surgery, Bo was there. When his wife, Gari, was in surgery, I was there. That's what authentic friendship looks like. It requires a commitment of availability of our time, energy, and resources. Few friendships develop this level of commitment.

Quality Three: Accountability

It is not easy to live according to the principles and commitments outlined in this book. It is human nature to drift toward mediocrity. We all need friends who hold us accountable and challenge us to be our best. We need friends who help us keep our belief systems, goals, and behavior on track. We need friends who love us enough to confront us when we need it. For nearly twenty years Jim Dixon has been that kind of a friend to me.

Allison and I moved to Colorado in 1975 so I could begin a master's program at Denver Seminary. I had met Jim at a friend's wedding in Kansas City the summer before. When we moved to Denver I needed a place to do my seminary field ministry, so I contacted Jim.

At the time Jim was the Director of Christian Education at Faith Presbyterian Church. He was willing to take a risk and let me teach an adult elective class at Faith. My teaching ministry eventually led to an internship at the church, which grew into a full-time job as Director of Adult Education. Jim moved into the position of Associate Pastor as his own preaching gifts began to blossom. Throughout the years I served at Faith Church, Jim was a constant source of encouragement and accountability.

In January of 1982 Jim, Bo, and I began the adventure of starting a new church. Since that time, we have had the privilege of serving the great group of folks that make up Cherry Hills Community Church. We have been ministering together almost as long as my wife and I have been married. During those years we have tried to hold each other accountable. When Jim is having a tough time, I know it. I try to be there to encourage and challenge him.

When I'm struggling, Jim knows it. He has always been there to challenge and encourage me. When we're both having a tough time, we go see a stupid movie together and try to encourage each other. That's what real friends are like. They hold each other accountable.[2]

Quality Four: Honesty

Authentic accountability requires honesty. In each of the relationships I've mentioned in this chapter there has been the common thread of a commitment to honesty. When I'm having a tough time and need someone to talk to, I know I can be honest with my friends. I tell them what is really going on in my gut and they tell me the same. In John Wesley's class meetings every member was required to tell the other members of the group the "true state of his soul" at least once a week. In obedience to James 5:16 they confessed their sins to one another and prayed for one another. That takes honesty.

Honesty requires hard work. Sometimes it means confronting our friends when we sense something is not quite right. This kind of honesty can produce conflict. Superficial relationships don't handle conflict well. Authentic friendships grow through conflict. "As iron sharpens iron," the Book of Proverbs says, "so one man sharpens another" (Prov. 27:17). "The kisses of an enemy are deceitful, but faithful are the wounds of a friend" (Prov. 27:6, author's own translation).

It seems that too often Christian leaders fall into sin and lose their ministry, or at least the sense of integrity that accompanied their ministry. I have the suspicion that these are men whose success has led to a degree of isolation. In isolation no one knew what was really going on in their lives. They didn't have friends with whom they could be truly honest. That is tragic. We all need the honesty that characterizes true friendship.

Quality Five: Confidentiality

An open and honest friendship requires a high level of trust. If I am going to share my struggles with a buddy, I need to have the confidence that what I share is not going to appear as a headline in next week's *National Enquirer*. Most people are not very good in this area of confidentiality. Nothing kills honesty in a relationship like a breach of confidence. Loose lips not only sink ships, they also sink fellowships. True friends know how to keep their mouths shut and hold confidences in confidence.

Quality Six: Regularity

Friendships, like all relationships, require the investment of time and energy. The friends I have grown close to are the ones with whom I spend time. I believe the reason many people fail to develop authentic friendships is that they fail to plan regular times of fellowship into their schedules.

I live in a busy metropolitan area. My life is filled with activity. I have more opportunities than time, so I have to make choices about how I spend my time. I must discipline myself not to be so busy attending to the urgent that the truly important gets neglected.[3]

I know that I need regular time alone with Allison; I schedule it. I also need regular time with Stephanie and Baker; I plan it. But I have also learned that I need regular time with a small group of men who provide me with a Grace's Place experience. I have learned to prioritize this time into my schedule. It takes quality time of consistent regularity to build authentic friendships.

Quality Seven: Prayer

Authentic friends pray for one another. I have no greater gift to give a friend than my intercession on his behalf in the presence of the living God. I want friends in my life who are committed to praying for me.

Several years ago I experienced a renaissance in this area of my spiritual life.[4] I try to spend a significant amount of time in prayer at least five days a week. I developed a notebook to help guide me and remind me of the issues I need to talk to God about during these times. One section of my notebook contains a list of the friends I am committed to pray for. When I get together with these men, we share with each other the needs and issues of our lives for which we desire prayer. We write these needs down and pray for each other. Over the years I have seen God do exciting things in response to the prayers of my friends. As I pray for them, and as they pray for me, our friendships deepen and grow more significant.

Proactive Friendship

Perhaps you have never had the kind of relationship characterized by the seven qualities of authentic friendship. If that is the case, you might be discouraged; you may believe you could never have such a friendship. Let me assure you, you can. Such friendships can be developed.

My friendships with Rich, Bo, and Jim developed naturally. I didn't have to invest a great deal of energy to make them happen. Then a strange thing occurred. I began to lose touch with them. Rich was living in another city which made consistent time together impossible. Jim and I were so busy with our different responsibilities at the church that we were rarely getting much time together. Bo had teamed up with a few other men to develop several new ministries. We were only connecting sporadically. The friendship component of my relational network was in bad shape, and I was feeling lonely and isolated.

I wish I could tell you that I was wise enough and exhibited the initiative to work on this area of need, but that is not quite how it happened. God, in his grace, was getting ready to teach me a lesson about how to develop friendships. I did take one highly proactive step. I began to pray that God would help me develop some new friendships. I believe that what happened in this area of my life was a direct answer to those prayers.

Without giving much thought to the implications of my actions, I started to think about forming a discipleship group with several men, guys that I wanted to get to know better. Several of these men were new Christians whom I thought I might be able to help in the process of their spiritual growth. I prayed about every person I thought ought to be in the group and then began to call to see if they would be interested in being part of a group. Every man God had placed on my heart responded enthusiastically.

We began meeting together in September of 1990. Our commitment was to meet regularly, every other week, at lunch time on Thursdays. Our objective was to tackle a discipleship program developed by the Navigators. The 2:7 series requires a commitment to memorize Scripture, cultivate a daily discipline of Bible study and prayer, and work to develop basic skills in ministry.

As our group spent time together an exciting chemistry evolved. Along with accomplishing the tasks to which we had committed ourselves, a spirit of camaraderie rapidly began to develop among the members of the group. Although I had the job of providing leadership for the group, I didn't look at our times together as work. I began to look forward to our Thursday meetings as a time to be with good friends.

One of the "grace" dimensions of the group was the choice of Thursday as our meeting day. As the Teaching Pastor at Cherry Hills Community Church my workload is heavily weighted on the front end of the week. I teach a Bible study for several hundred businessmen early on Tuesday mornings. On Wednesday nights I teach another large Bible study. These events are emotionally, physically, and spiritually draining. By Thursday I am usually shot! Shortly after our Thursday group started to meet, I began to experience serious emotional letdowns on Thursdays. I also was going through a period of discouragement in my ministry. Thursdays were becoming very difficult.

I shared with our group the struggle I was going through. The brothers rallied to my side. The men in the group became a tremendous source of support as I worked though this time of difficulty. The group was rapidly developing all the qualities of authentic friendship:

1. We met together in a spirit of unconditional love to help each other grow spiritually.
2. We made ourselves available to each other and sought to be there for members of the group who were having a tough time.
3. We were learning to be open and honest with each other.
4. We held each other accountable for spiritual growth and lovingly, yet firmly, encouraged each other.
5. We met together regularly.
6. We prayed for each other.
7. We joked around and had fun together, too!

We were becoming authentic friends.

The point I want to make is that this was an intentional group. It didn't happen naturally. It was purposefully planned and aggressively pursued. The result was the creation of authentic friendships. If you are weak in the friendship area of your relational network, you have the ability to develop authentic friendships. You might have an existing group of relationships that simply require a little work to develop into authentic friendships. Or there may be a group of men you have been wanting to get to know better that could be a group like the one we started. You might need to be the "point man" who leads the way.

If you think you lack the raw material for such a group, I would recommend finding a good church to join. If you are already a member of a good church, there is probably a group of men right in your church that could become a covenant friendship group. If not, you might consider looking around for a church where you can find this caliber of fellowship. If you work on this component of the ladder of love, you will soon discover your own Grace's Place where you can experience authentic friendship and find the encouragement and support you need to stay out of the Solomon Syndrome and off the Boulevard of Broken Dreams.

Personal Reflection

The friendship factor provides another place to stop and take a look at the priorities of your life. As you think about the following questions consider making the necessary adjustments. Doing so could build this area of your life into another vehicle through which your needs for love and meaning can be met more fully.

1. Who is the best friend you have ever had?
2. Do you have a Grace's Place in your life?
3. Are any of your friendships unconditional?
4. Do you have a friend with whom you can be open and honest?

5. Would you like to be held accountable in your spiritual life?
6. Pray that God would give you a few authentic friends.
7. Take action to start a small group.

10

Transcending Nonconformity

Turn Off, Tune Out, and Drop In!

In the summer of 1969 a half-million young Americans gathered on a farm in upstate New York for three days of "love, peace, and music." The original Woodstock has become legendary. On August 13 and 14, 1994 a group of aging baby boomer entrepreneurs attempted to re-create the "magic." This time nearly three hundred thousand members of Generation X (and a few ex-hippies) worked hard, with a great deal of apparent success, to capture the spirit of the sixties. That decade was a period in which multitudes of searching adolescents harkened to the call of Timothy Leary and "turned on, tuned in, and dropped out" in an attempt to make life meaningful.

The music at Woodstock was exceptional. The event was something of a mess. Let's face it; you can only stay high on drugs and alcohol so long while sliding half naked through the mud imagining that you've just found nirvana. Woodstock ended; nirvana was not attained. The optimism of the sixties led to the cynicism of the seventies and the apathy of the eighties. Nonconformity was not the answer.

Ironically, peace and love are exactly what we need to live full and healthy lives. They are not to be found, however, in substance abuse, casual sex, or even rock and roll. Paradoxically, these needs are only met as we leave behind a self-centered lifestyle and begin to practice self-extension through acts of service. This requires a relational commitment to the priority of our fellowman.

In 1979 folk singer Bob Dylan released an album entitled *Slow Train Coming*. One of the songs on that album reminded the listener that "you gotta serve somebody"[1] and specified that "it might be the Devil, or it might be the Lord, but you gotta serve somebody." We might not agree on every point with Mr. Dylan's theology, but the primary message of the song is indisputable. Life is about serving. The object of our service and the product of our serving will, to a great extent, determine whether our lives are fulfilled and significant, or shallow and meaningless.

Who is the happiest person on the planet? Who is the most joyful person in the world? It could be a very ordinary Albanian nun living in the slums of Calcutta. Agnes Bojaxhiu grew up in a comfortable home in Skopje, Albania. Those who knew her well during those days uniformly report that there was nothing exceptional about her. At the age of twelve she began to sense the call of God. In 1928, at the age of eighteen, Agnes joined the order of the Loreto Sisters and adopted the new name Sister Mary Teresa. In December of that year she sailed for India. Eventually, Sister Teresa became a geography and history teacher at St. Mary's school for girls in Calcutta.

St. Mary's was located on a spacious and elegant piece of property that was separated from the slums of Calcutta by high walls. In 1935 Sister Teresa began to regularly leave the walled security of St. Mary's to walk through the streets of Calcutta on her way to a second teaching assignment in the city. Those walks brought her into contact with the desperate plight of the poor in Calcutta. Eventually she would receive what she refers to as her "call within a call" to the poorest of the poor.

It is impossible for most of us to imagine what Mother Teresa saw on the streets of Calcutta. She saw unwanted babies abandoned on the street. She saw men and women literally rotting to death from leprosy. She saw the elderly left to die in the gutter. But she saw more than human suffering. In her own words, as I mentioned previously, she saw "Jesus in a distressing disguise." For over forty years Mother Teresa has responded to the call to leave the security of the convent behind to live and serve in the slums. She has learned the secret of serving her fellowman without expecting anything in return. What has this life of self-sacrificial loving and serving produced in her?

Several years ago British journalist Malcolm Muggeridge traveled to Calcutta to observe the work of the Missionaries of Charity firsthand. In his book, *Something Beautiful for God*, he describes how he discovered a remarkable group of women, living in the most meager circumstances, enveloped in an almost tangible atmosphere of joy.[2] Where do you find joy? It can never be acquired by the pursuit of physical pleasure. Joy is not a physical reality. It cannot even be attained by the quest for personal happiness. Happiness is a conditional emotional experience; true joy is experienced at a level far deeper than the emotions. Joy is a spiritual experience that only God can create in the human heart. It is a product of his work of blessing in our lives. It has a direct relationship to our acts of serving our fellowman.

Shalom

"Make me an instrument of your peace." This was the consistent and persistent prayer of Saint Francis of Assisi. Growing up in a wealthy home in Assisi, Italy, Francesco enjoyed all the advantages of wealth. He lived to be served. A trip to Rome in 1205 served as the catalyst that started a process of transformation in his life. He chose to respond to the call of God. Unlike the rich young ruler of Jesus' day, Francis renounced his worldly possessions and followed Christ in material poverty. His impoverishment led to spiritual prosperity. He spent the remainder of his life, like Jesus, seeking not to be served but to serve (Mark 10:45).

The great passion of Saint Francis's life was to be an instrument of God's peace. In the Sermon on the Mount Jesus taught the disciples "Blessed are the peacemakers" (Matt. 5:9). The priority of serving one's fellowman provides a wonderful opportunity for experiencing something of the blessing and joy that both Mother Teresa and Saint Francis discovered.

Peacemaking is rooted in the Hebrew concept of peace. The Hebrew word for peace is *shalom*. *Shalom* was much more than a greeting in the world of the Old Testament. It was a word that captured the essence of what a relationship with God could bring to a life. Peace, in the biblical sense, has a much broader meaning than our limited use of this word. When we use the word *peace* we are often referring to the end of hostility. In the sixties, flashing two fingers in the air expressed the desire of a generation to see the war in Vietnam come to an end.

But *shalom* (although it includes the idea of the end of hostility) is a much more comprehensive concept. The experience of *shalom* in the Bible is intimately related to God's blessing (see Num. 6:22–27). *Shalom* was a multi-dimensional concept that included material prosperity, physical health, emotional contentedness, relational harmony, and spiritual salvation. *Shalom* is a state of total well-being flowing from a proper relationship with God. It is a word that speaks of the quality of life that all men and women long to experience. Our role in dispensing *shalom* is a critical component in living a life that meets our own deepest needs.

Heroes

A peacemaker is a *shalom*-maker. Because of the multi-dimensional nature of *shalom*, peacemaking encompasses a wide variety of possible activities. Peacemaking is an attempt to be an instrument of God's *shalom*. It requires that we "tune out" the cultural bombardment that tells us to indulge ourselves, and "tune in" to the needs of humanity. It means "dropping in" by using the physical, emotional, spiritual, relational, financial, and political resources at our disposal to improve the quality of another human being's life. Peacemaking is a tangible expression of loving our neighbor.

Becoming a peacemaker requires a fundamental shift in our value systems. Our cultural paradigm indoctrinates us with a subconscious message to "love things, use people." If we are going to get serious about the priority of relationships, we must experience a paradigm shift that motivates us to "love people, use things." This is the underlying philosophical value system of the fellowman rung. It is the life philosophy of a peacemaker.

Peacemaking can take many different forms. Some of us have the ability to be physical peacemakers. By that I mean we can use our time, energy, and resources to improve the physical quality of another person's life. Others

among us are better equipped to be emotional peacemakers. We all have the potential to be used by God to be
spiritual peacemakers. God has uniquely created each of
us to play a peacemaking role in our world.

Peacemakers are often the unsung heroes of our world.
Maxine Jones is a hero. She runs a ministry called Manna.
Cherry Hills Community Church is located in the wealthy
Cherry Hills area bordering the city of Denver. It would
be easy for such a church to forget about the needs of the
poor, but Maxine makes sure that doesn't happen. On
Tuesday evenings Manna Ministries opens its doors. Orig-
inally started by Maxine as a food bank, Manna now offers food, clothing, medical care, and even free haircuts to
families in South Denver who are in need of a little physical *shalom*.

Sometimes the needs of our fellowman require more
than physical peacemaking. Dale and Alice Hudson are
two of my heroes. For nearly fifteen years Dale and Alice
have opened their home to foster children. Multitudes of
children have found a temporary home with the Hudsons.
Sensitized to the needs of handicapped children through
their daughter Dusty's struggle with cerebral palsy, many
of the Hudsons' "kids" have had unique needs that others have been unwilling to help with. Not only have Dale
and Alice provided a physical home, they have loved and
nurtured these children emotionally as well. Miracles happen in the Hudson home. A few "hopeless cases" have
graduated from college and are living productive lives because the Hudsons have been dispensers of emotional
shalom.

Rich Beach is a hero. For over twenty years I have seen
a nearly endless stream of spiritually destitute men and
women find new meaning in life through Rich's efforts in
the area of spiritual peacemaking. With a winsome personality and genuine concern, it is usually only a matter
of minutes into almost any conversation before Rich raises

the question of a person's spiritual condition. His sensitive boldness opens multitudes of doors. Where need and openness are present, Rich tastefully shares how to have a relationship with Jesus Christ. In restaurants, on airplanes, at shopping centers, and in nearly every imaginable arena of life, Rich leads people to Christ. The deepest spiritual needs of men and women are brought in touch with the *shalom* of God.

Gilman Hill is a hero. He is a petroleum geologist and physicist by training. Many years ago Gil struck a "deal" with God. Instead of living on 90 percent of his income and giving 10 percent to God's kingdom, Gil decided to live on the ten and give away the ninety. He even set up irrevocable trusts to ensure he didn't "forget" his "deal." Millions of dollars of spiritual, physical, and emotional needs have been met in the lives of people around the world because Gil is a peacemaker.

John Hicks is a hero. He is well educated and extremely sharp. John could do anything he wanted to. He would tell you with all honesty that he is doing just that. John runs a ministry in the inner city of Denver for schizophrenic street people. In John's words, he just "loves on them."

Dick Savidge is a hero. Hour by hour, day by day, he pours his life into the broken, fragmented, disillusioned, and distressed lives of the men and women who come through the doors of his counseling office.

These are the real heroes of our world. They are the hidden saints who improve the quality of life on our planet for countless multitudes. They are the peacemakers. Most of them are not much different than you and me. They have limited time and resources. Their weeks contain only seven days. Their mortgages are due on the first of the month. Their cars break down and their children need braces. So how do they do it? The answer lies in understanding that inside the value paradigm of every peacemaker you will find a commitment to the priority of his or her relationship with his or her fellowman.

Becoming a Hero

I have not shared the preceding illustrations in the hope that you would admire these men and women from afar. I have shared these stories to challenge *you* to become a peacemaker. Yes, you! You were designed and created to be an instrument of *shalom* in the life of your fellowman.

The Chinese character for the word *crisis* is a combination of two other Chinese characters. One is the character for *danger,* and the other is the character for *opportunity.* Our world is in a state of crisis. Our nation is in a state of crisis. Our cities are in crisis, our neighborhoods are in crisis, and often, our own families are in crisis. We are surrounded by crisis. But with the danger of crisis comes the opportunities crisis creates for peacemaking.

Never in human history have there been more opportunities to serve our fellowman. The danger most of us face is in becoming so overwhelmed by the scope of the need that we do nothing. In order to become effective as peacemakers, we need to sort through the multitude of opportunities available to us and focus our limited time, energy, and resources in areas where we can make our greatest peacemaking contribution. It is not enough to "visualize world peace." Living our lives with relational priorities requires us to become proactive in the peacemaking process.

If we go back to our diagram of the human motivational system we will see that out of our belief systems we set goals and take action. We do this every day in other areas of our lives. You probably have certain financial goals for your business and family. To achieve those goals, you have pursued a career. In some cases that career took years of preparation. Five or six days a week you roll out of bed and head to work. You act to achieve your goals.

Now you have a new goal. You want to serve your fellowman. At first this will be a broad goal. It will require that you treat people differently. It should affect the way you treat the people you live with, the people you work with, and the people you encounter throughout the day. Instead of viewing them as objects placed on the planet just to meet your needs and serve you, you begin to experience a paradigm shift. You look at them and seek to determine what their needs are and how you can serve them.

At times this process is quite obvious. Disaster strikes an African nation. The media gives the event headline attention and dramatic coverage. You see "Jesus in a distressing disguise" of hunger and poverty. Your heart is moved to compassion. You feel like you should do something. In the past you let this feeling fade without responding. Now it is different. You find an agency that is responding to the need in the name of Christ and write a check.

At other times the appropriate response is more complex. You are sitting in church and you hear about a great need for Sunday school teachers. You feel stirred and wonder if you should sign up. In the past you just ignored such pleas, confident that someone else would do it. How do you sort through the multitude of such situations you encounter? How do you discern the need from the call?

Discovering Your Gifts

The call to serve is not intended to be a call to attempt something you cannot do. It is intended to be a response to a task you have been custom-equipped to accomplish. When you made Decision One many wonderful transac-

tions took place in your life. You were invaded! Christ came
to live in you by means of the person of the Holy Spirit.
When the Holy Spirit invaded your life he endowed you
with supernatural abilities the Bible calls spiritual gifts.
The Bible says, "but to each of us gifts were given just as
he willed" (1 Cor. 12:11, author's own translation). The
spiritual gifts God has given us enable us to effectively
accomplish the tasks we are intended to accomplish.

Identifying Your Passion

Without going into great detail about how to discover
your gifts, a second dynamic of deciding where to invest
your serving energy is understanding that God gives us a
passion for what he has created us to accomplish. Our passion is intimately related to our person. Like snowflakes, no
two people on the planet are identical. Every man and
woman is an expression of the creative genius of God. We
might warp and distort the beauty, but each person's
uniqueness remains intact. God has providentially been involved in the development of your physical body, your personality, and your life experience. All these factors work together to create your passion. Certain needs and opportunities you encounter will "push your button" more than
others. These signals are important. They are part of how
God leads you.

Discerning the Call

No dynamic of serving our fellowman is more complex
and yet more simple than discerning the call of God. If
you have never sensed God's call on your life, it is extremely complex to attempt to describe this phenomenon
to you. Once you have experienced a sense of call, the phenomenon is so simple it requires no explanation.

At times God actually gives a call to service in an audible voice. This was true of the prophet Samuel at the time of Eli (1 Sam. 3:1–10). Usually, the call is not audible but internal. God engineers the circumstances of your life in such a way that you are exposed to the need that will become your call. Having been exposed to the need, you begin to have an inner stirring to see something done about the situation. That inner stirring begins to grow in your life. You sense that you are the one to do something. Somewhere deep inside you just know that God is prompting you. Someone has said that there are some things that you just "know in your knower."

When the call fits with your passion and your spiritual gifts, you can have confidence that you've found a place in which to serve your fellowman. You then must take action in the special arena God has designed for you. The Bible says that we are God's "workmanship" and that we have been created to accomplish good works which God has prepared in advance for us to do (Eph. 2:10). What a great picture! God prepares the work of serving. God then designs and creates the servant. He endows the servant with the abilities required to accomplish the work and then creates a passion in the servant's heart to see the work done. God places a call on the man to do the work and empowers the peacemaking enterprise with the enabling ability of his Spirit. When properly understood and experienced, serving is a no-lose proposition.

Don't be afraid to experiment. I have had to approach this subject conceptually, but in reality the unique gifts and ministries God has designed for you to accomplish are often discovered in the laboratory of trial and error. Like the Nike commercial, the message in this area of the network is "Just Do It!" Get involved. Find a place that fits your gifts, personality, and passion, and begin to serve.

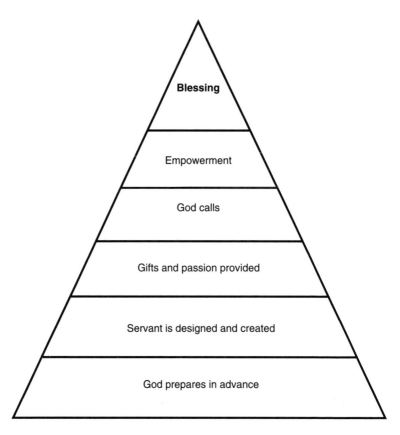

The result of these attempts will often be a sense of God's blessing in your life. It is a powerful experience to see how God can use your life to improve the quality of another person's life. Hopefully this act of serving will lead to others. Your peacemaking efforts will begin to give your life a new sense of purpose. You will begin to be a hero!

In an earlier chapter we saw how our sense of personal fulfillment is intimately related to the twin needs of security and significance. By developing loving relationships with the people in our prioritized network we will begin to build a source that meets our security needs. In turn,

Dynamics of Human Motivation

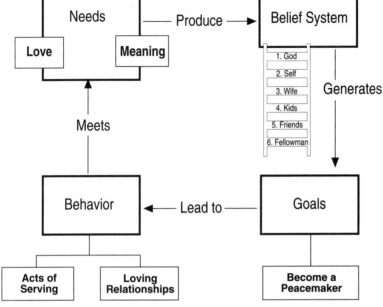

when we invest ourselves in acts of service to our fellow-man our need for significance will be met in new and un-expected ways. Here is the paradox of giving our lives away for the sake of Christ. In losing our lives for Christ's sake, our own deepest needs are met. We begin to discover the secret of lasting joy that Jesus came to model and teach. We put together a relational paradigm that keeps our lives from taking a trip down the Boulevard of Broken Dreams.

By now, perhaps, all these commitments and changes seem a bit overwhelming. Good! Does living this way seem impossible to you? Great! Does it all seem a bit unnatural? Let me assure you, it is! This is supernatural stuff; it re-quires a whole new source of ongoing enabling. If you're going to be a blessing, you need to be blessed. In the next chapter you'll get a few tips on how to make that happen.

Personal Reflection

Here are a few questions to reflect on and actions to take to help put the priority of the fellowman rung into action:

1. What are you doing in your life that gives you true joy?
2. Do you love people, or do you love things?
3. How could you become a peacemaker?
4. What needs in your church or community capture your interest? Could those needs be a part of your passion?
5. Ask God to make his call clear to you.
6. Step out and begin to serve somewhere. Trust God to guide your journey of serving your fellowman.
7. Look around. Don't overlook the obvious.

11

Getting Wired!

A Guide to Synthesis and Empowerment

A life built around a set of relational priorities can be extremely rewarding and fulfilling. It also has the potential to be unbelievably frustrating and discouraging. Our desire to live a more significant life will be rooted in a mind-set filled with good intentions. Most men have good intentions. I have never known a groom who entered marriage with the desire to fail. I have never met a father who embarked on the adventure of family life with the intention of neglecting or abusing his children. Most of the men I have talked with over the years about relationships have indicated that they would love to have healthy and vital friendships. Yet marriages fail, families crumble, friendships disintegrate, and the desperate needs of humanity remain largely unaddressed.

At the same time I do know men who have vital marriages, healthy families, meaningful friendships, and who are making a significant difference in the quality of life on the planet because of their selfless contribution of time, talent, and resources. The difference is not good intentions; it is often a matter of what I call synthesis and empowerment.

Synthesis is the product of a unifying principle or dynamic that ties all the areas of relationship together. Empowerment is the product of a source of enabling greater than ourselves. I know of only one adequate source of synthesis and empowerment that can make a lifestyle of relational priorities effective.

The Possible Impossibility

Several years ago I had an unusual and profound experience of enlightenment. Late one afternoon I was out on a walk to work out some of the frustrations of an exceptionally difficult day. I really don't remember the specifics of the day, but I do remember feeling like I had failed in the way I handled them. The more I stewed, the more frustrated I grew. Finally, I came to the conclusion that I was totally incompetent and inadequate to face life's demands.

As I walked along at an extremely brisk pace I began to say to myself, "I can't, I can't, I can't, I can't, I can't." My thought patterns fell into rhythm with my step. Although at first this was something of a dismal conclusion to my ponderings, eventually I began to sense a certain liberty in the experience. Suddenly, the truth of what I was thinking came into focus. *I can't!* That's the bad news. That is also the good news.

After some period of walking in the "I can't" mode I was reminded that living according to the divine design is always rooted in dependence on the empowering reality of the indwelling presence of Jesus Christ. In other words, *I can't* but *he can!* As this truth sank in I began to change the internal message I was repeating in cadence with my step. Suddenly, I was walking along subvocally repeating "he can, he can, he can, he can."

In a flash of enlightenment I realized that this little formula is the secret of empowerment. *I can't, he can.* In order to live a life of consistent spiritual and relational effectiveness we must learn to live in total dependence on the empowerment of Christ, made real in our experience by maintaining a vital relationship with him.

At the heart of this relationship is a radical transformation that takes place in the very core of our beings. Before making a decision such as Decision One of chapter 6 we were dead spiritually. The Bible refers to this reality when it says "you were dead in your sins and trespasses" (Eph. 2:1, author's own translation). The result of this reality is the warped way of living that I have referred to as the Solomon Syndrome. The belief system and mind-set produced by this syndrome is the product of a personality developed apart from the influence and empowerment of the Spirit of God. After making Decision One the Holy Spirit, absent before, is now present and dwelling in our inner beings. This is not only good news, this is great news!

When Christ makes us alive spiritually he begins a process of transformation which theologians call sanctification. This process has everything to do with our human motivational system. There are several dimensions to this transformation process.

The Bible tells us that we are transformed in part by a radical change in our thought patterns called "the renewing of your mind" (Rom. 12:1–2). Our old understanding of our needs and how to get those needs met is slowly replaced with the truth of God's revealed will for our lives. At first this is only cognitive information being processed by that funny gray matter in our cranial cavity. Over time, as the Spirit of God works in us, these truths make the critical eighteen-inch journey from our heads to our hearts.

The second phase of the transformation process involves implementing these new realities into our lifestyles and behavior. At this point we usually begin to experience another good news/bad news situation. A genuine attempt to live according to the priorities articulated in this book should prove to be extremely frustrating. That is the bad news. On the other hand, when we understand the concept of empowerment we will begin to realize that this frustration is also the good news.

Every once in a while I have a conversation with someone who is new to the life of following Christ. When he shares his struggle I say something like, "I have some good news and some bad news for you." I then go on to explain, "When you asked Jesus Christ to come into your life, he came. Jesus Christ is in you. That is the good news. The bad news is, *you* are still in you!"

The Bible refers to this reality as the struggle between the flesh (you in you) and the Spirit (Christ in you). It is normal to feel a bit schizophrenic. Every genuine, authentic, biblical, regenerate man has a "split personality." If you want a graphic illustration of what this looks like, go to the seventh and eighth chapters of the Book of Romans. Beginning in verse 14 of chapter 7 the apostle Paul shares his own struggle with living the spiritual life. The first time I read "I don't do the things I want to do and I keep on doing the things I don't want to do," I remember thinking, "Wow! Paul felt just like I do." In other words, Paul is saying "I can't!"

Unfortunately, many men never get past Romans 7. At the end of the chapter, Paul gives up. Then comes chapter 8. The entire eighth chapter is a discourse on living in dependence upon the indwelling power of the Holy Spirit. The message of the eighth chapter is "he can!" In these two chapters we see the secret of living the impossible possibility. Only by means of the supernatural enabling of the in-dwelling Christ are we able to live according to the divine design.

Blessed and Empowered

What is the purpose of our life? It is to love and to serve. In chapter 8, we found that the primary task of the father is to bless his children. I defined blessing as a touch of God that brings empowerment and wholeness on a life. There is a sense in which this is synonymous with loving and serving. We love with the love of Christ. We serve in the spirit of Christ. Our love and service become tangible ways in which God touches other people's lives to meet their needs.

Several years ago I taught a teacher training class called the Bethel Bible Series. The Bethel Series gives an overview of the Bible using pictures and key phrases. The phrase the Bethel Series chose to communicate the overall theme of the Bible is "Blessed to be a blessing." When we love and serve, with the love and spirit of Christ, we become a source of God's blessing. Blessing is the greatest need of our lives. When we are experiencing this touch of God on our lives we feel loved unconditionally and infinitely significant.

Notice that before we are able to be vehicles of blessing, we need to be blessed. The reason we are not effective in blessing others is often because we are not being blessed ourselves; there is no blessed father to bless his children, there is no blessed husband to bless his wife, and there are no blessed friends to bless one another in authentic fellowship. There are not enough blessed servants to meet the desperate need for blessing our fellowman. We need to be touched by God in a very real way that creates this experience of blessing. It is this reality that empowers us to live a relationally based lifestyle effectively.

Synthesis

We have seen repeatedly that if we are going to live in conformity with the purposes of God, the highest priority relationship of life must be our relationship with God. He is our source of power. He is the source of blessing. Our objective needs to be to live in a way that keeps us in the flow of God's blessing. For this reason, our relationship with God occupies the top position on the ladder of love. The quality of every other relationship in the network will to a great extent be a product of the quality of our personal, spiritual vitality.

The relationships of the network are interdependent. I have heard it said that if you really want to love your kids, love their mom. This statement reflects the fact that a higher priority marriage relationship will significantly impact the quality of the parent–child relationship. The prioritization of relationships within the paradigm reflects this reality. This principle can be illustrated by taking the ladder illustration and reconfiguring it into a series of concentric circles (see p. 163).

Notice that power and influence flow from the center outward. Reinforcement flows back to the center. The inner priorities determine the quality of the outer. The Christ relationship is central. It is the Christ relationship that empowers and influences every other relationship in the paradigm. Cultivating this relationship is of utmost importance if we are going to effectively live a spiritually centered lifestyle.

A Working Strategy

The walk I took at the end of a frustrating workday turned out to be a life changing event. After the walk I

Synthesis and Empowerment
In the flow of God's blessings

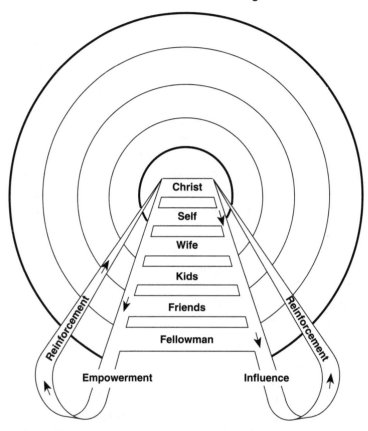

began to think about how I could keep myself in the "he can" mode with more consistency. I also wanted to figure out how to pass on to other men the truth I had discovered. As I thought about this challenge I was reminded of what a member of Alcoholics Anonymous once told me. I have always wondered why some men who join A.A. have tremendous results in their battle to overcome alcoholism while others seem unable to break the addiction. A friend told me the answer was simple. Joining A.A. is only one step in the recovery process. The real difference between recovery and ongoing disaster has to do with "working the program."

The genius of the A.A. approach to recovery is found in the "Twelve Step" program. The Twelve Steps give a man a simple daily strategy for recovery. If you work the program you will get better. If you don't, simply joining the organization will do you little good.

I immediately saw a direct analogy with the spiritual journey. Going back to the beginning of this chapter, you could again ask the question of what makes the difference between the guy who breaks free from the Solomon Syndrome and the one who continues down the Boulevard of Broken Dreams. In many cases the answer is a matter of whether or not a man has learned to "work the program."

I began to think through what a daily step-by-step working strategy might look like for men who were trying to put a spiritually based, relationally prioritized lifestyle into practice. I came up with a seven-step program for daily spiritual vitality.

Step One

The first requirement for working through this strategy is to set your alarm to go off fifteen minutes earlier in the morning. Find a place to be alone and get a hot cup of coffee. Find a modern translation of the Bible and have a notebook and pen handy.

The strategy begins with the acknowledgment of our need. This is the *I can't* step. It requires that we remember and embrace the truth that apart from the indwelling of Jesus Christ and the enabling power of the Holy Spirit, we don't have the ability to keep off the Boulevard of Broken Dreams. Begin by telling God something like:

"Lord, I am powerless. I can't be the kind of man you want me to be today without your grace and your help."

With that small acknowledgment you will have taken the first step toward a meaningful and significant day. It is amazing how coming to grips with this reality first thing in the morning will help get your day going in the right direction.

Step Two

Immediately after acknowledging your inadequacy, take the second step in the strategy by affirming God's adequacy. This is the *he can* step. Again, in an attitude of prayer tell God:

"Father, you are all-powerful. You have the ability to enable me to be the kind of man and live the kind of life that pleases you today."

I find that this affirmation is another great way to begin the day. It gets me thinking about how great God is and how much he loves me.

Step Three

The third step is the "plugging into the power" step. The experiential link in the entire spiritual enterprise is the indwelling of the person of the Holy Spirit. His activity in our lives enables us to do the things contained on the pages of this book. He needs to control, guide, and empower our day. Again, pray:

"Holy Spirit, I ask you to fill my life today with your presence and power. Live the life of Christ in and through me today."

These three steps get us spiritually postured to face the day in the power of the Spirit and live in a way we could never live without divine intervention.

Step Four

One of the dilemmas of living in relationship with God
is the old freewill problem. Wouldn't it be great if after
you took the first three steps you could just go out and
cruise through the day without any problems? Unfortunately, it doesn't work like that. Because you are a free
moral being, you have been vested with the ability to make
bad choices at any moment.

When you take the first three steps, you have, in effect,
dethroned self or ego from the control point of your life
and enthroned Jesus Christ as Lord. The key to living with
consistency, in the flow of God's plan, is maintaining this
internal position (with Christ in control and ego in sub-
mission to the Spirit). Step Four is a conscious step to invite Christ to reign as Lord over your life. It is as if you invite him to take control of the inner throne. This is a step
that might need to be repeated periodically throughout
the day as you become conscious that by an act of your
free will you have "bumped" him off the throne and
usurped his position at the control center of your life.
When you become aware that you have dethroned Christ,
you need to stop and pray something like this:

"Lord, I have blown it. I have dethroned you and taken
control again. I willingly step down and invite you to once
again reign as Lord of my life."

Step Five

Steps Four and Five of the program are "in the heat of
battle" steps. They will be helpful to review each morning so that you will remember them when you need them.
Step Five is a step that often needs to be taken when you
have usurped control again. Along with getting back into
the right relationship with Christ at such times, you need
to get honest with God and let him put his finger on

things in your life that are out of conformity with his will. It is a step that appropriates the forgiveness and cleansing made possible by Jesus' atoning death and resurrection. When you become aware that you need this step, pray:

"Search me, Lord, and show me where I'm offtrack. I turn from my self-centered sin and ask you to forgive and cleanse me."

Step Six

The sixth step in this daily strategy is a commitment to seek to grow in your relationship with Christ. You begin implementing this step the minute you set your alarm fifteen minutes early.

We have a variety of resources available to facilitate the vitality of our relationship with Christ. These resources are activated through the exercise of certain disciplines. There are four areas in which these disciplines need to be developed if the spiritual growth process is to provide the empowerment necessary to live out the relational paradigm. All four areas and their corresponding disciplines have the object of getting us "plugged into" Christ in a dynamic way. If we use them as an end in and of themselves they will become stagnant and unproductive. These are means to an end. The end is Christ himself.

Resource #1—The Bible

Communication is a critical component in every relationship. If we are to have an authentic relationship with God we need to experience a special process of communication. Most communication begins with spoken words. God has spoken. He spoke through the prophets. He spoke through the apostles. He spoke through the incarnation of the Son. The message of the prophets, the apostles, and the Son has been recorded for us in the pages of the Bible. No other book in all the world is like it. It is a "living and active" book (Heb. 4:12). Through this book God continues to speak. It is a powerful vehicle that plays a central role in our relationship with Christ.

To have a vital, productive, and effective spiritual life, it is imperative that we develop a consistent time of interacting with the Bible. Again, our objective in spending time alone reading the Bible is to encounter God and allow him to speak to us. For many men, setting aside time every morning or evening to read and reflect on the Bible has proven to be an invaluable resource in cultivating their relationship with Christ. Over time, as this relationship matures, we will sense God communicating with us as we spend time reading his Word. As we seek to live according to God's priorities the Bible will become our manual for life, the blueprint for meaning and significance.

When I first experienced my own paradigm shift I was skeptical about reading or studying the Bible. On several occasions I had picked up a King James Version of the Bible and started out on page one. It didn't take long before I found myself bogged down in some obscure genealogy. The book just didn't seem that exciting or relevant. After my encounter with Christ I received two very good pieces of advice about the Bible that I will pass on to you.

First, I was encouraged to obtain a copy of a modern translation. If the King James Version seems archaic to you it is because the King James Version *is* archaic. Many old saints, who have been reading the Bible for years, love the "thees" and "thous" of the King James Version. What many people don't understand is that this was simply the language of the common people at the time this version was translated.

If you are just beginning the adventure of cultivating a relationship with Christ I think you will find that one of the many good modern translations will help immensely in getting started on the exciting journey of exploring the spiritual truths and principles contained in this book. A clerk at your local Christian bookstore would be glad to help you choose a version that you find readable and enjoyable. The second tip is this: Start in the New Testament. Don't get me wrong; you will eventually find the Old Testament immensely helpful and quite fascinating. But to get off to a good start, begin by reading the New Testament. Start with one of the four Gospels. They contain the historical narratives of the life and teachings of Jesus. Try Matthew or Luke and then head on to John. Just a chapter a day will radically improve the quality of your inner life. Consider this a money back guarantee!

Set goals for yourself in this area. My personal goal is to spend a significant period of time reading and praying at least five days a week. These are often the best minutes of my day. All else is influenced by what happens in this time.

Resource #2—Prayer

Through reading, studying, and memorizing the Bible, God will begin to speak to us and transform our belief systems. But communication is a two-way process. We also need to speak to God. Through prayer we have been given this privilege. Along with time spent in the Bible, time in prayer is an essential means of enhancing our relationship with Christ.

Prayer is a form of communication with God. In prayer we move into a conscious experience of the presence of God. For many of us this means of growing in our spiritual life does not come naturally. We need to learn how to enjoy a more meaningful experience of prayer. Like the disciples, we have the need to come to Jesus and ask him to teach us to pray (Luke 11:1).

Jesus responded to the disciples' request by giving them a sevenfold pattern of prayer. Most of us are familiar with the Lord's Prayer as a rote, memorized, liturgical prayer. When used as an outline of seven topics, however, the prayer provides a helpful guide toward developing a more meaningful prayer life. I have dealt with this subject in depth in my book, *Transforming Your Prayer Life*.[1] For our purposes, let us briefly explore the seven components.

1. **"Father"** *(Relationship)*
   Begin your time of prayer focusing on God as your heavenly Father and consciously entering his presence.
2. **"Hallowed be your name"** *(Worship)*
   Prayer is a time to set our minds and hearts on the nature of God and give him praise and thanksgiving for who he is and what he does. Thank God for something he has done for you recently and praise him for some characteristic of his nature.
3. **"Your kingdom come . . ."** *(Intervention)*
   In prayer we have been given the privilege of appropriating God's intervention in our lives. Pray that the realities of his kingdom will influence your personal life, your family, your church, your nation, and the needs of the world.
4. **"Give us this day . . ."** *(Provision)*
   With Christ as our highest priority we are able to pray with confidence for God's provision in our lives. During prayer, set before the Father your needs, your desires, and all sources of anxiety in your life.
5. **"Forgive us our sins . . ."** *(Forgiveness)*
   Prayer is a time of getting honest with God. It is a time to wrestle with our flaws and failures and allow the grace of God to touch our lives with the cleansing work of Christ. Take a fearless moral inventory

of your life and get back on track with God's will and his plans.

6. "Lead us not . . . deliver us . . ." *(Protection)*
Living a spiritual life is a battle. We need protection from our own susceptibility to temptation and also from the hostile spiritual realities that seek to harm us. Appropriate the leading of the Spirit and the protection of the Father.

7. "Yours is the kingdom . . ." *(Affirmation)*
God doesn't need our affirmations, but we need to remind ourselves that *he* is in charge, not us. Close your time of prayer with a series of affirmations regarding God's sovereign authority over your life.

Over time, as you grow in your personal prayer experience, many other dimensions of prayer can be added to this pattern. This pattern is simply designed to help you begin to practice a discipline of prayer that will put you in touch with Christ on a daily basis.

Resource #3—Fellowship

The resources of the Bible and prayer are direct, vertical means of developing our relationship with God. But there are also horizontal resources that provide additional means of facilitating our spiritual growth. Fellowship encompasses all those relationships we enjoy with our fellow travelers on the spiritual journey. Since I have already spent a great deal of time exploring this dimension of the divine design in chapter 9, let me simply point out again how these relationships are interdependent. There is a synthesis that begins to take place when we operate from a spiritual and relational center. In fellowship we experience the reality of Christ's love as it is expressed through tangible, human vehicles. Authentic fellowship enhances our relationship with Christ. Our relationship with Christ enhances our human fellowship. Synthesis begins to develop.

Resource #4—Ministry

The ministry resource rounds out the picture. Ministry encompasses all those relationships of life with men and women who are not yet on the spiritual journey. Again, since chapter 10 was dedicated exclusively to this subject, I will simply point out that ministry to our fellowman has several benefits. Not only does it benefit the person being served, it enhances our relationship with Christ. Often we will feel that we have had more benefit from the act of service than the person being served!

With the centrality of Christ established and these four resources active in our lives, our relationships will begin to thrive. We will have access to the source of synthesis and power. Men who live with the ultimate priority of the Christ relationship have found the secret of living a life characterized by meaning, purpose, power, fulfillment, and eternal significance. Why wouldn't you want to live like that?! This leads logically to the final step.

Step Seven

The final step in the strategy is a commitment to seek to be a vehicle that Christ can use to influence the world for the sake of his kingdom. After spending these minutes getting plugged in to the person and power of Jesus Christ, you will want to get the rubber on the road. At this point in my own quiet time I often simply pray, "Put me in, Coach!"

As I began to use these seven steps as my own working strategy I became convinced that many men needed a simple tool like this to keep their days productive and spiritually vital. I began to expand these steps and explain them in written form. The result was a book entitled *Daily Disciplines for the Christian Man.*[2] If you need more help with the above suggestions, I would recommend that you obtain a copy.

I believe that if you work on cultivating this priority of your personal relationship with God, everything that we have explored together in this book will begin to come into focus in a wonderful and exciting new way in your life.

Personal Reflection

Your relationship with Christ is the most important area of your life, and you need to submit it to consistent assessment and adjustment. This relationship is one that I try to take a look at daily. As you seek to develop your relationship with Christ, here are a few questions to reflect on and a few suggestions about actions you can take:

1. What in your life is a source of synthesis and empowerment?
2. Set aside fifteen minutes a day for five days this week to read a chapter in the Bible. Begin with the Gospel of Luke.
3. Try using the seven components of the Lord's Prayer to pray five days this week.
4. How does your marriage affect your children?
5. How does your spiritual life affect your marriage?
6. What keeps you from developing the basic disciplines?
7. Obtain and read *Daily Disciplines for the Christian Man.*

12

Swords, Staffs, and Peggy Sue

The Secret of Finishing Well

As the old adage goes, "All good things must come to an end." What is true of all good things certainly applies to life itself. For those of us who consider ourselves to be in the prime of life it is difficult to imagine that one day our lives on this earth will be over. At eighteen we live like we are indestructible. At thirty we begin to notice weird things happening to our bodies. By forty time seems to pass by at an accelerated pace. When we hit midlife our mortality and frailty come crashing in upon us in not-so-subtle ways. If we are lucky enough to live a full life, one day we will be in the unique position of looking back at the years and making some kind of an appraisal of how they were spent.

Over the last twenty-plus years I have had the pleasure of being involved in the lives of many men who are making the transition from living according to the defective value system of contemporary culture to a life based on the priorities of the divine design. Twenty years ago most of the men I worked with were young and at the beginning of their careers and family lives. Today, I spend a great deal of time with men who are either going through midlife transitions or heading into late adulthood. One of the consistent concerns I hear from these men is the desire to finish well.

It has been said that most men do not finish well. How tragic to come to the later years of our life and find that the systems and approaches that served us well in our youth really don't work well in later life. Newspaper and television reports seem filled with the accounts of men who have not finished well. What does it take to come to the later stages of life and look back with a sense of satisfaction that your life has counted for something that is self-transcending?

The View from the Bridge

In recent years behavioral scientists have given much attention to what has become known as adult life cycles. The forerunner of these recent studies was the work done by Erik Erikson at Harvard University in the late sixties. While working as Professor of Human Development at Harvard, Erikson published a book entitled *Identity: Youth and Crisis*.[1] In this work Erikson attempted to map out the stages of human development from birth to death. He theorized eight successive stages of human development and identified the major tasks that needed to be accomplished during each of those eight stages. The possible outcomes of attempting to negotiate these tasks provided the titles for each of the stages. The eighth and final transition period Erikson labeled "Integrity vs. Despair."

Erikson observed that men who reached this final stage of life tended to look back and make some assessment of their lives. This assessment produced one of two conclusions. Either they achieved a sense of what Erikson called integrity, or they developed a sense of what he called despair.

Erikson found that in order to achieve a sense of integrity, three tasks needed to be accomplished. First, he found that a sense of integrity seemed to be rooted in the development of a series of relationships that produced *intimacy*. Second, he found that men needed a sense that through their lives something of value was being passed on to the next generation; Erikson called this task *generativity*. Finally, he found that integrity was a product of what he called *ideological commitment*, by which he meant living one's life on the basis of a meaningful value system.

If, on the other hand, a man's life was characterized by *isolation* rather than intimacy; and if instead of generativity one sensed that nothing of value had been passed along to the next generation (what he called *stagnation);* and if, rather than ideological commitment, a man lived with what Erikson called *confusion of values*, then the assessment would likely be one of despair. These observations, by the way, were not made in a religious context; they were the conclusions of an expert in the field of human development at one of our nation's leading universities.

Ten years after Erikson's book was published a team of researchers from Yale University published *The Seasons of a Man's Life*.[2] Daniel Levinson headed the team and the project about which the book reported. This particular study focused on the adult life cycles of men. Taking an interdisciplinary approach, Levinson and his team identified three major periods of adulthood. The final period was called "late adulthood." Levinson observed that during this period each person has an experience that he called "the view from the bridge." Like Erikson's final stage, this period was characterized by a time of appraisal in which men make some assessment of their lives. Levinson saw the goal of this assessment to be the discovery that one's life has been meaningful and valuable. According to Levinson, such an appraisal is necessary in order to face death with a sense of integrity. Levinson's findings were identical to Erikson's. Both were perfectly consistent with the blueprint for living contained within the divine design of God's revealed plan we have explored together in this book.

For those of us who are familiar with the main themes of the Bible, there is nothing new in the work of either Erikson or Levinson. Almost 3,500 years ago a man by the name of Moses wrote, "Teach us to number our days aright, that we may gain a heart of wisdom" (Ps. 90:12). Moses understood the importance of living with a sense of perspective. He knew that one day he would stand on the final "bridge" of life and look back. It seems as if Moses was praying that the view from the bridge would be good, and the final assessment would be one of integrity and fulfillment rather than one of despair. Nothing could be quite as tragic as to arrive at the end of our lives feeling this sense of despair and knowing that there was no solution to our dilemma.

Images of Despair

After reading both Erikson and Levinson I began to reflect on the lives of biblical characters who modeled integrity and despair. Perhaps no historical figure more personifies the tragedy of despair like King Saul. Saul was the first king of the United Kingdom of Israel. He was a man who got off to a great start. Chosen by God himself, Saul was anointed to be king by the prophet Samuel. The Bible tells us that the Spirit of God came upon Saul and he led the armies of Israel to great victories over its enemies. At the age of thirty Saul was on track. Unfortunately, the rest of his biography is the story of one man's decline into despair. Acting presumptuously, Saul violated God's guidance given through Samuel. As God began to withdraw his blessing from Saul, another man (by the name of David) appeared on the scene. Saul responded to David's growing popularity with intense jealousy. In fits of rage Saul even tried to murder David. His attempts to rationalize his blatant disobedience were met with one of the great rebukes of biblical history when Samuel proclaimed, "To obey is better than sacrifice, and to heed is better than the fat of rams" (1 Sam. 15:22).

Finally, God revealed that he was going to take the kingdom away from Saul. Saul began to experience episodes of what modern psychiatry might diagnose as manic depression. In desperation, and with serious value confusion, Saul resorted to witchcraft and sorcery to find guidance.

The final scene of Saul's life was dismal. It can be found in the thirty-first chapter of 1 Samuel. Saul was seventy years old. The army of Israel had been totally defeated. Saul's sons lay dead around him. In total despair Saul leaned on his own sword and committed suicide. He left nothing behind but a life characterized by isolation, stagnation, and a total confusion of values. The view from the bridge was bleak. He did not finish well!

Images of Integrity

In contrast, the Bible also contains many images of lives characterized by integrity. One such image is found in what at first glance might have been a life voted "Most likely to finish in despair." Jacob didn't have a great start.

Although he was the son of the patriarch Isaac and the grandson of Abraham, Jacob was a scoundrel from birth. He came out of the womb jockeying for position and trying to maneuver into the place his older brother rightly held as the firstborn. He manipulated his brother into selling his birthright for a bowl of soup and tricked his father into giving him the blessing reserved for the firstborn. Having thoroughly swindled his brother and father, he was forced to flee Canaan to save his life. This flight was the beginning of a pilgrimage for Jacob that would eventually bring him back to Canaan a changed man.

Jacob fled to the home of his Uncle Laban (who was quite a scoundrel himself!). Jacob was about to get a healthy dose of his own medicine. Laban had a daughter who was a real knockout. Her name was Rachel, and Jacob fell hard for her. He contracted with Laban to work seven years for the hand of Rachel in marriage. After seven years the big day finally came. Jacob went into the dark tent to consummate the marriage. There was only one problem: The next morning he found Rachel's sister Leah lying next to him instead of Rachel! Apparently, Leah wasn't quite as cute as Rachel (the nicest thing the story has to say about her is that she had "weak eyes"). Laban justified his actions and talked Jacob into another seven years of work to get the girl he wanted in the first place.

Through a series of similar experiences, God used the circumstances of Jacob's life to begin to change him. Finally, the day came when Jacob headed back home, hoping to be reconciled with his estranged brother. The climax of this journey, and of Jacob's life, took place when he reached the banks of the river Jabbok (see Genesis 32). Jacob sent his family, his servants, and all his flocks across the river while he stayed behind to do business with God. That night Jacob wrestled with the angel of the Lord. He refused to quit wrestling until he received God's blessing.

The prophet Hosea gives us an important insight into the nature of Jacob's wrestling. He tells us that Jacob wept and begged for the angel's favor (Hosea 12:4). Jacob's real struggle was not with God, it was with himself. God was wrestling with Jacob on Jacob's behalf. We are told that the angel of the Lord blessed Jacob, but that he also wounded Jacob for life. Jacob's relationship with God was changed, and with it, the course of his life. The staff that Jacob would need to walk would be a constant reminder of what God had done in his life (and of his dependence on God to meet his needs). From that night forward Jacob was a different man. He began to live his life on the basis of ideological commitment instead of his old value confusion.

The final scene of Jacob's life should be a source of encouragement to those of us who find it easier to relate to a character like Jacob than to many of the other heroes of the Bible. When God changed Jacob's character he also changed his name. Jacob became Israel. He was the father of twelve sons who became the heads of the twelve tribes of Israel. At the end of his life we see Jacob being used to bless the Pharaoh of Egypt, his twelve sons, and even his grandsons. In the final moments of his life Jacob "worshiped as he leaned on the top of his staff" (Heb. 11:21). What a great picture of a life that ended in integrity! He had served God, he had loved and been loved, and he left behind a godly heritage that would affect generations to come. The view from the bridge was good; he finished well!

Those two men provide vivid images of the view from the final bridge of life—Jacob leaning on his staff and Saul leaning on his sword. One is an image of integrity, the other an image of despair. One man discovered how to live according to the divine blueprint; the other locked into the Solomon Syndrome and traveled down the Boulevard of Broken Dreams. How can we be sure we finish well, leaning on a staff instead of a sword?

The Bottom Line

In his book, *The Seven Habits of Highly Effective People*, Stephen R. Covey writes that people who want to live in a way that really counts need to cultivate the habit of beginning with the end in mind.[3] He encourages the reader to imagine his own death and funeral, and even challenges him to write his own eulogy as given by a member of the family, a close friend, and a member of the community. In a sense he is encouraging the reader to project himself into the future and decide what he wants the view from the final bridge to look like. Once you know what you want the end to be, you can then begin to make the choices necessary to achieve that end.

One day, unless Jesus returns first, you and I are going to die. Ultimately, our eternal destiny depends on our relationship with Christ. If we have received Jesus Christ's gift of forgiveness we do not need to fear judgment. But one day we will have a personal assessment to make. It will be the self-evaluation of our lives. We will each have to face the final view from the bridge. On that day I believe the questions we ask ourselves will be quite simple.

Question One

Our first assessment will be an evaluation of whether or not we have developed intimacy. "Have I loved and been loved?" will be the first question we will ask. "Have I loved and been loved by God and other people? Have I made relationships the priority of my life?"

Question Two

We will also evaluate what we are leaving behind. "Have I left a godly heritage?" will be the second question. We live in a time and culture that places a great deal of value on the practice of leaving an inheritance. Unfortunately, little emphasis is placed on the practice of leaving a heritage. Someone has said that the correct answer to the question "What did he leave behind?" is "Everything!" In eternal terms the answer to that question might tragically be "Nothing!" Are we building a godly heritage that conforms to the paradigm?

James Dobson tells the story of a woman who left a great heritage for her son. Dr. Dobson was doing rounds on the cancer floor of Children's Hospital in Los Angeles. During his rounds he met a little five-year-old boy who was dying of lung cancer. In the words of Dr. Dobson, it doesn't get much worse than that! But that little boy had a mother who really loved him. Every day when Dr. Dobson went by the room, the boy's mom would be holding her little boy on her lap and singing to him to help ease his pain. One day as Dr. Dobson walked by the room he heard the little boy talking about "hearing the bells." He concluded that the little fellow must be close to the end.

Later that day when Jim ran into the boy's mother he told her about the incident. The mother began to laugh good-naturedly and told Dr. Dobson that her boy wasn't hallucinating. She told him that she had taught her son that when it was time for him to die, Jesus would come to take him home, and that he would know it was Jesus if he heard the bells of heaven ringing for him. "Those were the bells of heaven, not a hallucination," she said. Later that day the little boy died in his mother's arms as she rocked him and sang to him. I don't know if this mother could have left her child much of an inheritance, but I promise you this: At five years of age he already had a heritage that took him through the worst life had to dish out![4]

Question Three

The final question we will ask from the bridge is "Have I served God?" The image of the view from the bridge is profound. Death really is a bridge; it is the final bridge that leads to our eternal destiny. In that instant nothing will be as important as the answer to the question "Have I served God?"

The answer to the questions asked from the bridge will be the product of how well we have assessed and adjusted our priorities. Every small assessment is leading us to the big assessment of this final bridge.

One evening recently Allison and I decided to stay home and rent a flick. We picked up a movie called *Peggy Sue Got Married*. The movie is the story of a woman who goes to her twenty-fifth high school reunion at a very difficult time in her life. Things are not working well. Her husband has just run off with another woman. Her self-esteem is at an all-time low. At the reunion she faints and awakens to find herself back in her senior year. Peggy Sue has just traveled back to the age of eighteen, *but* she has retained all the knowledge and experience she possesses twenty-five years later. The thesis of the movie is developed around this theme: What would you do if you could do it all over again knowing what you know now?

Standing on the bridge in the twilight of their lives, many men will wish they could have just such a chance. In that moment will *we* wish we could go back and do things differently? The problem, of course, is that we can't go back; it is impossible. We can live our life any way we choose, but we can only live it once. We make the choice: integrity or despair.

God's desire for our lives is clear. He has planned for our integrity. He has given us a plan for living well. The relationships reflected in the ladder of love are the best he has to give. His plans and purposes are intended to enable us to develop a blueprint for happiness. If followed, they will help each of us live a life that is meaningful and fulfilling; they will lead us to a moment when we will cross the bridge into eternity to live forever in a perfect loving relationship with God. The view from the bridge will be good!

He Who Wins

Life is precious. Life is short. It is too short to spend our years living in futile ways that will never meet the deep needs of our lives. The choice is ours: the defective paradigm of a fallen culture or the relational paradigm of a loving God, the Solomon Syndrome or the divine blueprint.

Have you ever seen the bumper sticker that says "He who dies with the most toys wins"? That is the lie of the cultural paradigm. My daughter recently acquired a No Fear T-shirt that has much better "theology and geometry." The back of her shirt bears the motto "He who dies with the most toys still dies!"

I'll tell you who really wins. He who has a great relationship with God when he dies, that's who wins. He who has a rich and mature marriage that has weathered the storms of life and has survived the years, that's who wins. He who has a family that is healthy and vital because he made the tough choice that time with his kids was worth the cost, that's who wins. He who is surrounded by a group of friends who love him and are willing to go to the wall for him, that's who wins. He whose life has been meaningful and significant because he learned how to escape the myopic land of self and to invest his time, energy, and resources improving the quality of life for his fellow human beings, that's who wins. These are the real issues of life. These are the choices that determine the quality of our existence, now and forever. This is what God's plan for our lives is all about. It offers an alternative to the Solomon Syndrome, a set of values and priorities that are guaranteed to make you a winner in the biggest game of all: life.

Personal Reflection

As you come to the end of this book I encourage you to spend some time reflecting on the major components of the relational network and assessing how well you are doing in building a life structure that will make you a winner. Here are several ideas to help you accomplish such an assessment:

1. Go back and review the questions at the end of each chapter and review the suggested actions that accompany the questions.
2. With one of the illustrations of the relational paradigm in front of you, evaluate which area of the network is your greatest strength and which area needs the most work.
3. If you are married, ask your wife to assess your greatest area of strength and greatest area of need.
4. In prayer, ask God to show you what you need to do to get your life more in harmony with divine priorities.
5. Share what you are discovering with a friend. Consider giving a copy of this book to a friend and discuss it with him.
6. Brainstorm a list of actions you need to take to get your priorities in order.
7. Say "no" to at least one activity this week that takes you away from time with people in your personal paradigm.

8. Continue to read good books related to all areas of relationship (that is, marriage, family, friendship, spirituality, etc.).
9. Live a long, good, productive, meaningful, satisfying, and blessed life!
10. Finish well!

Notes

Chapter One: Boulevard of Broken Dreams

1. John Kennedy Toole, *A Confederacy of Dunces*. New York: Grove Press, Inc., 1980.

Chapter Two: Life's Too Short to Drive a Chevy

1. John Denver, "Blow Up Your TV," from his album, *Aerie*, R.C.A. Records, 1971.

Chapter Three: The World According to Tripper Harrison

1. Stephen R. Covey, *The Seven Habits of Highly Effective People*. New York: Simon and Schuster, 1989.
2. *Meatballs*, Paramount Pictures, 1981.
3. Douglas Adams, *The Hitchhiker's Guide to the Galaxy*. New York: Crown Publishers, 1980.

Chapter Four: We Are Who We Think Other People Think We Are

1. Abraham H. Maslow, *Motivation and Personality*. New York: Van Nostrand Reinhold Co., 1954.
2. Lawrence J. Crabb Jr., *Effective Biblical Counseling*. Grand Rapids: Zondervan, 1977.
3. Robert H. Schuller, *Self Esteem: The New Reformation*. Waco: Word, 1982, pp. 33–35.
4. David A. Seamands, *Healing for Damaged Emotions*. Wheaton: Victor Books, 1981, p. 103.

Chapter Five: Buckets, Ladders, and Paradigm Shifts

1. *Westminster Confession of Faith: Drafted by the Westminster Assembly, 1647.* The Shorter Catechism: Question One.

Chapter Seven: Making Love Last

1. Tom Robbins, *Still Life with the Woodpecker.* New York: Bantam Books, 1980, p. 112.

2. "The Chemistry of Love," *Time,* February 15, 1993.

3. John Cougar Mellencamp, "Jack and Diane," from his album *American Fool,* Riva Records, 1982.

4. Malcolm Muggeridge, *Something Beautiful for God.* New York: Harper and Row, 1971.

Chapter Eight: Buy a Harley!

1. Gary Smalley and John Trent, *The Blessing.* Nashville: Thomas Nelson, 1986.

2. Edith Schaeffer, *What Is a Family?* Grand Rapids: Fleming H. Revell, 1975.

3. "The Origins of Alienation," *Scientific American,* August 1974.

4. *The Family Gone Wild* is available through your local Christian bookstore for rental.

5. Smalley, p. 49.

6. Ross Campbell, *How to Really Love Your Child.* Wheaton: Victor Books, 1977.

Chapter Nine: Hanging Out at Grace's Place

1. Louis Evans Jr., *Creative Love.* Grand Rapids: Fleming H. Revell, 1977.

2. For more information see my small booklet, *Accountability Among Men,* published by NavPress, 1994.

3. For a discussion of the urgent versus the important see Charles Hummel's booklet, *Tyranny of the Urgent.*

4. For more help in the area of developing your prayer life see my book, *Transforming Your Prayer Life.* If your bookstore can't obtain it, call (303) 781–0091.

Chapter Ten: Transcending Nonconformity

1. Bob Dylan, "You Gotta Serve Somebody," from his album *Slow Train Coming,* Sony Records, 1979.

2. Muggeridge, op. cit.

Chapter Eleven: Getting Wired!

1. Bob Beltz, *Transforming Your Prayer Life*. Brentwood, Tenn.: Wolgemuth and Hyatt, 1991.
2. Bob Beltz, *Daily Disciplines for the Christian Man*. Colorado Springs: NavPress, 1994.

Chapter Twelve: Swords, Staffs, and Peggy Sue

1. Erik H. Erikson, *Identity: Youth and Crisis*. New York: W. Norton and Co., 1968.
2. Daniel J. Levinson, *The Seasons of a Man's Life*. New York: Ballantine Books, 1978.
3. Covey, p. 95.
4. James Dobson, from a story told in Denver, Colorado, in the late seventies.